WHAT'S MY **BABY** THINKING?

Practical child psychology for modern parents

WHAT'S MY BABY THINKING?

Tanith Carey

Clinical Psychologist
Dr Angharad Rudkin

CONTENTS

Foreword 6

Our philosophy 8
A good enough parent 10
Your baby's brain 12
How babies and toddlers learn 14

Baby development 16
Toddler development 18
Connecting with your baby 20
Your world post-baby 22

CHAPTER 1
Your 0–6-month-old

What can my baby see? 26
What does the world feel like to my baby? 28
Why does my baby move their body like that? .. 30
Parents' survival guide Adjusting to prematurity 32
Why does my baby startle so easily? 34
How does my baby know how to feed? 36
What can my baby hear? 38
Parents' survival guide Co-parenting 40
Why is my baby always hungry? 42
Why does my baby grip so hard? 44
Why does my baby stick our their tongue? 46
Parents' survival guide Co-sleeping 48
Does my baby recognize me? 50
When will my baby stop crying? 52
Can my baby tell night from day? 54
Parents' survival guide Babies and sleep 56
What is my baby staring at? 58
Can my baby recognize their own name? 60
Has my baby started smiling? 62
Why does my baby try to roll over? 64
Parents' survival guide Touch 66

CHAPTER 2
Your 6–12-month-old

Why does my baby suck on everything? 70
Why does my baby babble? 72
Why does my baby love to be held in the air? ... 74
Why does my baby love bath time so much? 76
Parents' survival guide Introducing
    solid foods 78
Why is my baby crawling like that? 80
What words can my baby understand? 82
What does my baby see in the mirror? 84
Why does my baby like nursery rhymes? 86
Parents' survival guide Twins 88
Why does my baby find that funny? 90
Why does my baby love peekaboo? 92
Why does my baby drop food? 94
Parents' survival guide Play 96
Why is my baby now afraid of strangers? 98
Why does my baby point at everything? 100
Why does my baby love to bang and clap? 102
Why does my baby hate nappy changing? 104
Why doesn't my baby want to come
    off the breast? 106

CHAPTER 3
Your 12–18-month-old

Parents' survival guide Creating a sense of safety 110
Was that my baby's first word? 112
Why does my toddler love "Let's Pretend" games? 114
Why does my toddler make so much mess? 116
Parents' survival guide Memory 118
Why does my toddler only want my partner? 120
Why is my toddler so fascinated by animals? 122
Parents' survival guide Separation anxiety 124
Why does my toddler love pressing buttons? 126
Why won't my toddler give up their dummy? 128
Why won't my toddler eat their dinner? 130
Parents' survival guide Walking 132
Why does my toddler say no all the time? 134
Why is my toddler refusing to go to sleep? 136
Why does my toddler have a favourite toy? 138
Parents' survival guide Travel 140
Why is my toddler so sensitive? 142
Why does my toddler want the same book? 144
Why does my toddler love to take risks? 146
What do my toddler's scribbles mean? 148
Parents' survival guide Christmas and birthdays 150

CHAPTER 4
Your 18–24-month-old

Why won't my toddler share? 154
Is my child old enough to have a friend? 156
Why does my toddler hate being left at nursery? 158
Why does my toddler think their toys are real? 160
Parents' survival guide Introducing a new baby 162
Why does my toddler hate going in the pram? 164
Why is my toddler so jealous? 166
Does my toddler understand how I feel? 168
Why does my toddler bite and hit? 170
Parents' survival guide Tantrums 172
Why does my toddler keep stopping on our walks? 174
Why won't my toddler wear their coat? 176
Why does my toddler hate brushing their teeth? 178
How does my toddler see colours? 180
Parents' survival guide Potty training 182
Why does my toddler love to sing and dance? 184
What do numbers mean to toddlers? 186
How fast is my toddler learning new words? 188
Parents' survival guide Bilingual babies 190
Why is my toddler fascinated by my phone? 192
Why does my toddler have so much energy? 194
Parents' survival guide Screen time 196

Bibliography 198
Index 204
Acknowledgements 207

FOREWORD

Your baby came into the world as a tiny miracle. While they may be in need of your constant protection, they are already a powerhouse of potential. Your child arrives as a raw bundle of emotions, looking to you as their caregiver to help them make sense of their exciting new life.

When you tune into what they need and help them ride the waves of feeling when they are hungry, tired, or alone, you are laying the strong foundations for lifelong emotional wellbeing, too. The care you give your child in the first two years has the greatest impact of all. We're fortunate to live in a time when we've never known more about how babies and toddlers think and develop.

We also know you're busy. Working as a team – myself as a parenting author and Dr Angharad Rudkin as a child clinical psychologist (with five children between us), we have set out to tackle, without fuss, fluff, or bias, nearly 80 situations you will meet in these key years, in a format that makes this the easiest-to-use book for parents of babies and toddlers ever written. As adults, we no longer consciously remember what it was like to be an infant or young toddler, but we are so lucky that we now have an incredible body of research which allows us to see the world as they see it. Over time, this will allow you to have a deeper appreciation of your child as a unique individual. At a time of life when your child has so few ways to express themselves, this understanding will make them feel loved and valued – a lifelong gift.

In modern life, there are many things that can throw a parent's natural intuition off course. Competitive culture, social media comparison, parenting trends, as well as stressful lifestyles, can undermine your confidence. This book gives you the knowledge to trust the process. When you step into your child's world, you will be able to join with – and enjoy – their voyage of discovery and give your child the space they need to unfurl from defenceless newborn into the expansive, confident toddler they are meant to be.

TANITH CAREY

Becoming a parent is part of nature, but it doesn't always feel natural. It is a journey of learning, challenges, growth, and joys. With information at our fingertips comes an expectation that we will know everything at the right time, leaving parents unsure, or striving for a perfection which doesn't (and shouldn't) exist.

What's My Baby Thinking? gives you information based on the latest evidence, and offers you an insight into not only your own thoughts and feelings but also those of your child. This is what parenting is – a dance between you and your child for the rest of your life. Moving with them, knowing when to step away or lean in, changing as they change, and understanding how to differentiate between their perspective and yours.

Learning about yourself as you learn about your baby in these first two years can sometimes feel relentless and difficult, but it can also provide immense delight and comfort. I wish you all the best as you start your own precious journey into parenthood.

DR ANGHARAD RUDKIN

OUR PHILOSOPHY

You and your child are on a voyage of discovery. As they explore the world, you are the companion they need to witness their wonder. Our guiding principle in this book is that what children want most is to feel safe with the adults who care for them.

This means tuning into your child's feelings and looking for cues to help meet their needs. Babies don't have the words or experience to interpret their emotions, so they "act" out how they feel.

If our minds jump to words like "naughty" when our toddler has a tantrum, these labels separate us from what our child really needs: to feel calm, safe, and regulated again. In today's competitive world, we tend to focus on stimulating babies' brains, and we often forget that their nervous systems are also at a critical stage of development. Babies come into the world in "survival mode" with underdeveloped nervous systems.

We now know from neuroscience that over time, attentive and empathetic parenting changes the way this gets "wired up". If babies are often held and soothed, this releases feel-good bonding chemicals – giving them feelings of contentment and safety, calming the over-reactive survival response. If babies and toddlers are left alone in distress, levels of stress hormones keep circulating in their bodies. If this often happens in the first two years, it can change the way a child's nervous system develops – keeping stress levels high.

Of course, it's never going to be possible to meet your child's every need, every time. But it's also not possible to hold a baby "too much" or "spoil" them. When you soothe them when they are upset with a calming voice, slower breathing, and with gentle smiles and touch, this gives signals to their developing nervous system that everything is OK, not just now, but in the future.

FOUR PILLARS OF PARENTING

Model the behaviour you want to see
As soon as they come into the world, your child or toddler is watching you. Whether it's sharing with others or talking in a respectful tone to your co-parent, model the behaviour you would eventually like to see.

Regulate yourself first
Your child will regulate themselves more easily if you are regulated. So, in trickier moments, if you feel yourself go into a fight-or-flight state, get in the habit of taking a moment to pause, breathe, and ground yourself. Notice when you are starting to feel overwhelmed. View asking for help from other caregivers, so you can refill your cup, a sign of strength, not weakness.

Name your child's emotions
When we see our children express uncomfortable feelings, like anger or jealousy, as loving parents we often want to talk them out of them or tell them not to feel that way. Don't be afraid of these emotions, try to brush them under the carpet, or tell your child what they "should" feel. Instead, help them name the feelings, even before they are saying their first word, as they will sense your empathy and understanding. Giving them a "feelings vocabulary" will help them process their emotions throughout their lives.

You're in charge
As part of their exploration of the world, there will be moments when your toddler will experiment with the boundaries you give them. Rather than seeing our children as small tyrants deliberately trying to make our lives difficult, it helps if we see them for what they really are: small children learning to deal with powerful feelings. It may seem that they want to be in charge, but they are really looking to you to manage their emotional states. Avoid the slide into seeing it as a battle of wills. Be secure in your leadership.

A GOOD ENOUGH PARENT

Today's parents feel the pressure to be perfect for a range of reasons. Social media has created a culture of comparison – and debate – over the "right" parenting style. This can leave modern parents wondering if we're getting it "wrong".

It might sound contradictory, but one of the best ways to be a good parent is *not* to try and be "perfect". This is the basis of "good enough" parenting – a term first used in the 1950s by the English paediatrician and psychoanalyst Donald Winnicott, which has gained widespread support by child development experts ever since. It describes the need for parents to be the "secure base" who meet a child's basic emotional needs by giving them enough emotional and physical care so they can grow into healthy, well-adjusted adults. Today, we tend to think we have to excel at everything – so "good enough" now tends to sound mediocre or average.

However, this is not the case in parenting, where being "good enough" is an emotionally healthy approach to a challenging job. "Good enough" parenting recognizes that we all have our good days and bad days. Trying to be perfect doesn't help, because it's an unattainable ideal that just creates stress and anxiety. It's not good for your bond because when you inevitably don't achieve perfection, you will feel less confident and as if you are "failing" your child. In fact, what helps your child to thrive is if you are less hard on yourself and more relaxed about being with them.

Embrace imperfection
Trying to be perfect also sets up an unhealthy example for your child. Winnicott argued that if we meet our child's needs every single time, they never learn how to cope by themselves if they feel sad, bored, or frustrated. Equally, beware of the pendulum swinging the other way, thanks to social media trends which give the message that it's OK to view young children as "little monsters" who can never be satisfied, so it's not worth even trying. Even before they have the words, your child will pick up that they are an annoying "inconvenience" to you.

> **BETTER PARENTING IS WHEN YOU TAKE THE TIME TO ENJOY BEING WITH YOUR CHILD. THIS MAKES THEM FEEL TRULY LOVED.**

Remember it's possible to feel many different feelings about parenting at the same time. Feeling tired, bored, or frustrated from time to time isn't a sign you are not a "good enough" parent. It's the natural consequence of a non-stop job where you put another person's needs before your own most of the time.

When babies are too young to talk, parents tend to judge themselves according to objective measures, like their weight, how long they sleep, or how soon they can sit up or crawl. But babies are who they are for many reasons, not just your parenting skills. Be aware of the "shoulds" that might creep into your thinking – possibly advice from others who have their own personal histories or unexamined beliefs about childhood. Listen out for the inner critic who tells you you're not doing it "right" – and be prepared to contradict it with a more compassionate voice. According to Winnicott, it is enough to be confident that you are really trying to do your best.

While it's impossible to do parenting "perfectly", better parenting is when you take the time to enjoy being with your child and giving them your undivided attention. It's this which makes them feel truly loved. It's the intimate connection you have with your child – and how well you tune into them – that matters, not how your parenting skills look to the outside world.

YOUR BABY'S BRAIN

Imagine the development of your baby's brain as a house under construction. When your baby is born, their brain already has its own basic external structure: the walls and the doors are already in place.

This framework has all the raw materials to make it spectacular inside – including over 100 billion brain cells – but a huge amount of wiring needs to be done to get it fully up and running.

The foundations

When your baby was born, the foundation of your child's brain was also in place. This is the primitive lower part necessary for our basic survival and life systems. Known as the limbic system, this area includes the amygdala – which looks out for danger and triggers the fight-or-flight response. The lower brain is also the source of our basic emotions, like anger and fear.

As your baby grows, the upper floors of their brain are also under construction. The cerebral cortex, the outer layer of the brain, is where they will do their more sophisticated "higher thinking". As humans reproduced over the course of millions of years, this part of the brain was the most recent part to evolve. It includes structures like the frontal lobes, behind our foreheads, responsible for much of our intelligence, rational thinking, decision making, and planning. For the first years, this upper floor is a work-in-progress.

Over time, through your child's experiences and interactions, these bottom and top layers link up and start to work together, almost as if there is a staircase between them. Gradually your child will gain more control over raw emotions and impulses that come up from the bottom floor – and learn how to manage them.

Connecting the left and right sides

Throughout childhood, there is another major piece of construction work taking place. Like a double-fronted house, your child's higher brain has a left and right side. For most people, the left side is where we think more logically and organize our speech and thoughts. The right is where we register emotion and recognize more nuanced verbal and non-verbal communication. These two halves connect via a "corridor". This is the corpus callosum, a bundle of fibres that runs between the two sides. Although it starts to develop in the womb, the most intensive building work of this corridor happens when your child is around two, though it will continue until your child's mid-teens. The wider and bigger this corridor becomes, the more your child can freely access both sides and gradually gain control over their feelings.

Wiring your child's brain
The wiring in the house is under rapid construction. Your baby's brain cells need to be linked via synapses – or connections – allowing messages to pass. At the peak of their brain development, these are growing at the astonishing rate of two million every second.

To start with, this wiring is not very efficient and the messages move slowly. But over the coming months and years, they become insulated with a waxy fat called myelin, which allows the messages to travel more rapidly. The most obvious way you will see this is that your baby's movements become more coordinated and smoother as they grow. You will notice when your baby goes from making jerky limb movements as a newborn to having the coordination to smoothly reach out and grab objects by about four months old.

Completing the "house"
It won't be until adulthood that your child's "house" is eventually built. Of course, within these floors, there are many separate "rooms" – or sections – with different functions. If you watch out for how different parts of your child's brain start to work together, you will start to see how they begin to master control of their bodies and their emotions.

HOW BABIES AND TODDLERS LEARN

Your baby is born hardwired to understand how the world works. Free play, different experiences, and interaction with you are their best teachers. Give them space, freedom, and encouragement to foster curiosity – a lifelong asset.

Learning through experience
At birth, your child's brain is a jumbled mass of cells waiting to be wired up. Over time, millions of these neurons are connected and the links between them strengthened by repetition, trial and error, imitation, and problem-solving.

To start with, your baby learns about the world through their senses. The first time your child puts a wooden block in their mouth, different parts of their brain registered the taste, feel, and weight of it. Next, when they build a tower with that block, they learn about cause and effect, and then gravity, when they keep knocking it over. Every time your baby does this, neurons fire, forming synaptic connections between their brain cells and thickening their higher thinking cerebral cortex.

At first, your baby doesn't know the coloured cube they like so much has a name – because your words sound indistinguishable. Over time your child is able to pick out the syllables you say often when you give it to them – and work out that this object is called a "block".

The importance of curiosity
From birth, you will notice your baby is always experimenting with cause and effect – whether it's watching how a toy sways when they swipe at it to watching what happens when they drop food off their highchair tray. As they play, your baby's concentration span will gradually get longer.

Between seven and 12 months, your baby will be able to focus on a toy for a few seconds. With your encouragement, by 19 to 24 months they will be able to focus on a plaything for up to three minutes. This ability to focus is the foundation of their learning and knowing.

Why repetition is key

Throughout these early years, repetition is key to helping your child learn. For example, singing the same songs, reading the same books, or playing the same games helps their neural circuits form in the brain and become stronger. Even though repetition can feel boring to an adult, for your baby it's the cornerstone of their learning.

Familiarity gives them "scaffolding". When they know what is coming next, they gradually build up new layers of understanding based on what they already know. For example, they may ask for the same animal book again and again. It may feel the same to you, but every time your child looks at it, they are building their understanding. Once they have got used to repeatedly turning the pages to see the colourful images they remember from last time, they can learn next what the characters' names are, what they do, and how they might think and feel.

Getting on the move – and more

As your child starts to be able to point, crawl, walk, and then run, they will now hit another learning milestone. They will develop autonomy, which means they are more in charge of their world and how they move in it. They will be able to seek out

> **FROM BIRTH, YOU WILL NOTICE YOUR BABY IS ALWAYS EXPERIMENTING WITH CAUSE AND EFFECT.**

objects they are interested in and ask you to name them. As you talk about them, your toddler is starting to join the dots on how the world works.

Now they can isolate what they see, and hear it labelled, and find out more about it, there will now be a dramatic explosion in their vocabulary. At 18 months, the average toddler will say about 50 words, though they can understand a lot more. By their second birthday, this will have risen to between 100 and 200 words.

With every word they learn, they will be able to communicate their needs – eventually helping them to form their first friendships.

Building long-term memory

This vocabulary explosion means that your child is then able to tell stories about their lives in words. Memories before this point are embedded in their life experience and everything they have become and know how to do. But now their newfound ability to describe events in their lives helps them embed more facts and events. This kind of longer-term memory is the foundation on which all their future learning is based.

BABY DEVELOPMENT

In their first year, your baby will go through a remarkable transformation. By the time they turn one, they will be on the move and starting to make their first words.

0–6 MONTHS

Thinking
Your baby's brain is about a quarter of its adult size. At first, they are experiencing the world via the senses of touch, sight, smell, and hearing. The first emotions your infant experiences are based on the release of different chemicals and hormones into their brain's nervous system, like cortisol and adrenaline when they are hungry, tired, or stressed, and oxytocin, serotonin, and dopamine when they are fed and comforted.

Relating
The world appears in shades of grey to your newborn, who sees most clearly at a distance of 20–30cm (8–12in). This helps them focus on your face when they are held in your arms. By six months old, they can see several yards across the room and in full colour. Your newborn will turn their eyes in the direction of your voice, which they remember from the womb. By six months old, your baby will immediately recognize you by sight and sound. Even very young babies will gaze at your mouth trying to work out how you form words. By six months old, they have developed enough control of their mouth and tongue to babble and try to imitate sounds you make.

Doing
When they are laid on their back, your newborn baby will place their head to one side. By three months, they have developed the neck strength to hold their head straight and push themselves up on their arms when on their fronts. Between three and seven months, they can roll over and, after that, crawl.

At first, your new baby will only clasp objects as a reflex. By between three and six months, they have developed enough control and coordination of their hands to reach out and grasp things they are interested in. By six months, your child's spine is strengthening, helping them to sit up for longer, with support from a pillow or your hands.

6–12 MONTHS

Thinking

Now their vision has improved and they can see clearly, your child wants to explore more of their surroundings by getting on the move, whether by rolling, crawling, or pulling themselves up to stand. By around eight to nine months, if you hide a toy in front of them, your child will now look for it, because they know it still exists, even though they can't see it.

While they may not be able to say the words yet, your child will increasingly show their understanding of what you are saying, with gestures, like waving when you say, "bye bye."

Relating

Now your baby has developed such a firm attachment to you, they are more wary of people they don't know. They may cry when you leave them with others.

After experimenting with babbling, your baby now starts to use the noises they make to get your attention, with sounds such as shrieks. Your child can point with their index finger, so will now start to point to direct your attention to things they want to show you.

Doing

Your baby can sit up without as much support, so they can use their hands more to grasp objects and bring them to their mouths to explore them. Between nine and 12 months, your baby can make use of their thumb and forefingers in a more delicate pincer grip to pick up small objects, like pieces of food, which they can put in their mouths. Your baby will use their new manual dexterity to make things happen – like striking their highchair tray with their hands to make a noise.

TODDLER DEVELOPMENT

Over the coming year, your child is likely to go from walking to running and climbing – and they will be bursting to use their developing skills to explore and test their newfound independence.

12–18 MONTHS

Thinking
Now on the move, your toddler is more of a little scientist than ever. They want to try out cause and effect and are curious to see what happens if they push over their block tower or open and shut cupboards.

They will now have a set of favourite books that they enjoy reading over and over. As their memory starts to get better, they look forward to seeing the pictures on the following pages and predicting what will happen next. Your toddler may now enjoy having a comfort object, like a favourite toy, or a piece of blanket, to carry around, because it's familiar or it reminds them of you.

Relating
During their second year, your toddler will be starting to say their first words – usually things they see or hear most and which are made up of simple syllables that are easier to say. By the end of this year, they may be learning as many as eight to 10 new words a day.

Your toddler may say "No", even when they don't mean it. Often, it's the easiest way to express the feeling that they don't want to do something, or they want to test their independence. Your toddler can now act on simple instructions, like "Give me the cup".

Doing
Your toddler's gait will develop from waddling to walking with their arms up to taking longer, faster, narrower steps forward, with their arms by their sides. Their limbs are lengthening, and their head becoming more in proportion to the rest of their body, making balance easier, and walking and running more confident.

Improving coordination between different brain regions means their motor skills are expanding. They are starting to kick balls and throw them, underhand and later overhand.

18–24 MONTHS

Thinking
By the age of two, a child's brain is about 75 per cent of its adult size. The frontal lobes, which govern reasoning, emotions, and memories, are developing quickly now, so they are starting to remember more. Now your child can start to name and use objects, they are interested in playing out what they see in more complex "Let's pretend…" games.

Your child wants to test their independence, but is learning that's not always possible, resulting in feelings of overwhelm and tantrums.

Relating
Your toddler can't yet imagine what other children their age think or feel. This means they will tend to play alongside their peers in parallel, rather than play with them. Children this age are racing ahead with language. By their second birthday, they're likely to have a bank of between 50 and 200 words – and can understand many more than they can say. As their language develops, they may start repeating the last few words of a phrase you just said – known as echolalia – until they start forming more of their own sentences.

Doing
Your child will delight in running and starting to jump. With help, they will be able to walk up and down stairs by putting both feet on each step.

From being able to make simple lines and marks with a crayon grasped in their fists, by the end of their second year your toddler can probably make more controlled marks and rough circles.

CONNECTING WITH YOUR BABY

As you stroked your bump, your baby learned to recognize the pressure and speed of your touch. As you spoke, they learned to recognize your voice. At birth, your baby was just as eager to meet you as you were to meet them.

As you gazed in wonderment at them, they were already scanning your face, and looking at you when you spoke. This mutual curiosity – and attempt to understand one another – is at the heart of your connection with your child.

How connection develops
This bond will quickly build as your baby learns that you and your co-parent are the people most likely to pick them up when they cry – and make them feel safe. Every warm and positive interaction between you is deepening your attachment to one another.

Touch is a vital part of your connection. When you hold your child close, it releases the feel-good bonding hormone oxytocin into both your bloodstreams. When you are relaxed and cuddling together, your breath and heart rates will synchronize, and you will "co-regulate".

Mirroring each other

From the outset, your baby tries to mirror you. If you watch carefully, by two to three months, you will see them smile back at you, look where you look, and stick their tongue out when you do. Before they form words, they babble to mimic the cadence of your speech. Imitating one another and sharing interests is one of the strongest ways to connect. You are giving your baby the message that what interests them is important. This will encourage them to keep seeking connection with you.

Why play bonds you

Playing offers countless opportunities to connect. In play, your child welcomes you into their world. To join them there, be an equal partner and let them be the director. Avoid correcting them, so they feel confident to suggest new games. Weave play into your day. Nappy changes, mealtimes, and journeys can all be opportunities. In play, you share laughter, which is another way of saying, "We like the same things" – long before your child can say their first words.

Building on that bond

You may feel connected with your baby the moment you set eyes on them – or you may need more time. Instead of seeing them as a bundle who just needs feeding, burping, and nappy-changing, see them as an individual already trying to connect with you. It may be as fleeting as the way they gaze at you and watch your face, a frown crossing their brow, a different cry, or the way they wave their arms. By viewing your child as an individual with their own feelings, your relationship will begin to grow immediately. Every loving response makes an impression at this time of rapid brain development.

Your child may not consciously remember this period of their lives, but the sensation of being consistently loved and cared for creates their Internal Working Model. This is how your child feels about themselves – and how they expect to be treated by other people now and for the rest of their lives.

Your relationship beyond babyhood

While every relationship is two-way, your child shouldn't have to act or behave a certain way to win your smiles – or your approval. They want you to delight in them for who they are. For real connection, allow them their full spectrum of feelings too, even the ones that feel uncomfortable or inconvenient for you.

Your child will feel more connected to you if you try to understand all their emotions – not just the ones that make you feel good. This will help them feel that they are enough, and acceptable to you as they are. The message you will be sending is that you are always on their team, no matter how they feel. Though it may seem a long way off, in future years, your child will feel more able to be open and vulnerable with you – essential for real connection.

YOUR WORLD POST-BABY

Just as your baby is becoming their own independent feeling human, you are also going through a process of becoming a new person. As you watch your child discover their new world, that's just part of the story. You are entering a portal to huge psychological and physical changes.

Research has found that after they become mothers, women's brains change permanently, especially in the regions involved in social and emotional processing. And we now know that hormone levels in fathers also change when they have children, to help them become more caring and empathetic. Instead of only focussing on your child's progress, celebrate how much you are growing and learning, too.

Time to reframe
You'll be surprised by the earthquake of parenthood, whether it's how little time you now have to yourself, how your priorities change, or how quickly you forget what life was like before.

We often hear how stressful parenting is, rather than how rewarding. After all, you are meeting the constant needs of another human being who relies on you for everything. But we also live in an era which often makes it more stressful than it needs to be. For example, the constant interruptions of the digital world can interfere with the flow and connection between us and a new baby. It can confuse even very young children into thinking our screens must be more interesting than they are.

Many of us combine child-rearing with working. Two working parents may not have a "parenting village" or a close network of family to share the load – as has been the norm for millennia. In our drive to support our little ones and provide for them materially, it's easy to forget that anxiety is contagious and that we, the parents, set the emotional thermostat in our homes.

Build your village
You cannot do this alone. You were never meant to. Human children were meant to be born into a tribe in which all members looked out for their welfare. Whether it's grandparents, siblings, aunts and uncles, or close friends, invite other carers into your life to give love and care to your child.

> **THE THINGS YOUR BABY MOST WANTS FROM YOU – CHATTING, SINGING, CUDDLING, SOOTHING, AND PLAYING, ARE ALL FREE.**

Time to simplify

The things your baby most wants from you – chatting, singing, cuddling, soothing, and playing, are all free. While you will never get more hours in the day, it is possible to prioritize what you do have. When in doubt, default to this simple question: "What does this feel or look like to my baby?"

Put your own oxygen mask on first

Focus on your own emotional state just as much as theirs. When you are calm and regulated, your baby is more likely to be too. If you are often stressed, they will be too.

Create a sliding scale from 1–10 in your head. Let 1 mean: "I'm feeling relaxed" and 10 "I'm feeling burnt out." Work out where you stand. When it gets to 6 or 7, it's time to refuel, by raising your hand and telling your partner or other caregivers: "I need some help here."

Being on the same team

The most important thing you can give your child is not an immaculate nursery or designer baby clothes. It's caregivers who give them a sense that their home is a trusted place.

If you are raising your child with a co-parent, it's also important to nurture and meet the needs of your relationship. Let go of any expectation of having a "perfect partner" too, as it can lead to criticism that can have a corrosive effect on your relationship. Relieve the pressure on one other to get everything right.

Be interchangeable as caregivers so that if one of you is taking a break, the other can easily slip into the other's shoes. Plan a weekly date night, even if it's 20 minutes stargazing out of the window together. Be direct but respectful in your communication and express your core needs rather than get lost in the detail. After all, you have a common, overarching goal – raising a child who feels safe and loved.

CHAPTER 1

YOUR 0–6 MONTH-OLD

"WHAT CAN MY BABY SEE?"

Vision is the most complex of the human senses and takes the longest to develop. When your baby first arrives in the world, it will look grey and blurry to them.

SCENARIO | When your newborn baby is awake, you notice they seem to gaze intently at you.

As your baby grew in your womb, there was little to see. For your baby it would have been like being in a dimly lit room with the curtains closed. Because your baby grew in the dark, their retinas – the layer of cells at the back of their eyes which process light – are still undeveloped at birth. The neural circuits in their brain that will make sense of what they see also have a lot of linking up to do.

As your newborn starts to look around at their new world, what they see starts to stimulate the visual cortex, bringing this complex system online. After birth, the colour-perceiving cone cells in the retina will also start to quickly develop. This means that gradually your baby will go from seeing the world as fuzzy and monochrome to sharp and in colour by the time they are about six months old.

WHAT YOU MIGHT BE THINKING

Can they actually see me? After nine months in my tummy, there's so much for my baby to look at.

WHAT THEY MIGHT BE THINKING

- **The cones** in the middle of your baby's retinas, which process colour and detail, are not yet fully developed. For now, your baby will mainly see the world as blurry and in shades of grey.

- **At first**, your baby sees best at 20–30cm (8–12in), about the distance when you look down at them in your arms. This helps them screen out too many new experiences and concentrate on getting to know your face.

- **The rods** at the outer edge of their retinas are better developed, so your newborn will trace the outline of your face first when they look at you or at new objects close to their face. This allows them to work out the basic shapes of things.

- **Because their eyes** are attracted to edges, your baby's gaze will be drawn to contrasting patterns, such as black and white stripes with sharp definitions.

SEE RELATED TOPICS
Does my baby recognise me?: pp.50–51,
What is my baby staring at?: pp.58–59

> **AFTER BIRTH, THE COLOUR-PERCEIVING CONE CELLS IN THE RETINA WILL QUICKLY DEVELOP.**

HOW YOU COULD RESPOND

In the moment

Show contrasting colours
As your baby is always looking for outlines, show them books and toys in black and white, which they can focus on more easily.

Help them track objects
The muscles controlling the focus and movement of your baby's eyes are still weak. When your baby is awake and alert, help their eye muscles get stronger by slowly moving a toy back and forth near their face, so that they can follow it with their eyes.

In the long term

Place objects within their peripheral vision
Hold new objects and hang mobiles just to the side of your baby at first, so they can see them more clearly.

Switch feeding sides
To help your baby develop their vision equally in both eyes, feed them on both sides so each eye has a turn at being dominant as they look up at your face.

Give them natural light
Your baby's eyes need different intensities of light, and to see objects at varying distances, to develop good vision over the coming months. To help with this, try to take your baby outside in daylight every day.

"WHAT DOES THE WORLD FEEL LIKE TO MY BABY?"

When they are born, your baby is so underdeveloped that, for now, they experience the world via raw inputs to their lower brain from their five senses.

SCENARIO | As you gaze at your newborn, you wonder what this strange new world outside the womb feels like to them.

Babies don't yet have the cognitive development to have "thoughts". Instead, they experience the world through their senses of touch, taste, smell, sight, and sound, which they have been developing in utero. These messages from the outside world trigger the release of chemicals into your baby's body. If your infant feels safe, warm, and well-fed, this releases feel-good chemicals, like oxytocin and opioids, helping them to feel calm and regulated. If they feel frightened, that will release stress chemicals such as adrenaline and cortisol, which will make them feel anxious and dysregulated. These feelings will trigger crying, as a way to seek your protection and feel calmer again. With experience, your baby will start to notice what makes them feel safe or unsafe.

WHAT YOU MIGHT BE THINKING

What's going through my baby's mind?
They are so tiny and helpless. All these new sights, sounds, and smells must be overwhelming.

WHAT THEY MIGHT BE THINKING

- **The first thing your baby notices** when they are born is that they are no longer held snugly by the warm, elastic walls of the uterus, and that the outside world is cold and exposing. So, their first instinct will be to reach out for your touch, so they feel safe and warm again.

- **Thanks to their advanced sense of smell**, your baby will quickly recognize – and be calmed by – the smell of your skin. If you are breastfeeding, they will also recognize the taste from the amniotic fluid that surrounded them in utero.

- **Over the last few months in the womb**, your baby has been able to hear your voice, even though it was muffled. Babies have good hearing as soon as they are born, and will be instantly comforted by your speech, which will sound familiar.

- **Babies are wired by evolution** to be instantly drawn to their main caregiver. They will gaze at your face as an early way to connect with you.

HOW YOU COULD RESPOND

In the moment

Make your baby feel safe
To a newborn, birth is a shock. Research has found that recreating the sensations of the womb can help soften their adjustment to the outside world. Remember that it's impossible to "spoil" a baby by holding them "too much". Carrying babies gives them a sense of safety at the most helpless time of their lives.

Help them find their hands
Your baby has been sucking on their fingers for comfort for many weeks in utero. Moving their hands up to their mouths will help recreate that sense of security.

In the long term

Return their gaze
Your baby will stare at your face intently in the hour after they are born and when they are alert and awake. Hold their gaze and start the first to-and-fro of communication by smiling and talking to them. Your eye contact lets them know they are important to you.

Keep talking
Your baby will use their eyes to look in the direction of your voice soon after birth. Keep giving them the reassurance of your presence by singing, talking, and reading to them, even though they don't yet understand the words.

Look for signs of overwhelm
Lots of stimulation from the outside world, like light and noise, can be too much for your baby. This will show up as fussiness, crying, or looking away. Look out for clues they are overstimulated and need a more peaceful environment.

SEE RELATED TOPICS

Why does my baby startle so easily?:
pp.34-35

"WHY DOES MY BABY MOVE THEIR BODY LIKE THAT?"

At first your baby does not have full control of their limbs, which seem to move erratically. Over the coming months, they will learn to move their bodies more smoothly and deliberately.

SCENARIO | When your newborn is alert and awake, you notice they move their legs in a stepping motion and wave their arms for no apparent reason.

After birth, your baby must learn that they are a separate person from you, with a body of their own. They don't fully understand that the arms, legs, feet, and hands they see moving in front of their eyes are attached to them. For now, they mainly move in response to raw messages from their nervous system, which is still so young that the messages are erratic, making movements look jerky. The motor areas of the brain also need time to wire up to their muscles before they are under control. As the messages between brain and body start to run more smoothly, this quivering will fade.

WHAT YOU MIGHT BE THINKING

Why do they move their limbs like that? They move so randomly, especially when they get upset and start crying.

SEE RELATED TOPICS
Why does my baby grip so hard?: pp.44–45

WHAT THEY MIGHT BE THINKING

● **Even though your baby's movements may look random,** they are helping build the feedback loop between the motor cortex in their brains and their muscles.

● **If your baby feels tired, hungry, or upset,** their more visible limb movements are a way of alerting you that they want to be held close.

● **Until they gain more control,** many of your baby's movements will be pre-wired responses to stimuli, like the rooting reflex.

● **At first, your infant's movements are jerky** because the nerve fibres carrying messages between their brain and muscles are not coated with myelin, a fatty substance that supports smooth movement.

> YOUR BABY MUST LEARN THAT THEY ARE A SEPARATE PERSON FROM YOU, WITH A BODY OF THEIR OWN.

HOW YOU COULD RESPOND

In the moment

Read other cues
If your baby is flailing their limbs and the cause is not clear, look for what might be bothering them. Are they also rooting – a clue they might be hungry? Are they turning away from light – a sign they might be overstimulated? Are they drawing their knees up to their tummy, a sign they might have gas? To help regulate their nervous system, turn down the lights and offer milk. Cuddle them, cradling their arms and legs close to you. Give your baby time and as they experience your warmth, smell, voice, and heartbeat, they are likely to start to calm.

Try swaddling
Before birth, your baby got used to feeling snug in the womb. It may help some newborns to relax and settle if they are swaddled – wrapped in a thin breathable fabric from the shoulders down – for their first few weeks. Avoid wrapping too tightly and watch for cues they find it restrictive or annoying.

In the long term

Flex their limbs
When they are playful, give your baby space to strengthen their limbs while lying on both front and back. The more they stretch their legs and arms and discover how it feels to move them in space, the earlier they will learn to reach, grab, and kick objects.

Use a baby gym
Kicking or swiping at a toy above them will help them learn that when they touch an object with their bodies, they make it move. As they discover this cause-and-effect, they will start to make movements more purposefully.

Check their body language
Your baby will bring their fingers to their mouth for comfort or if they are hungry, or use their hands to block out light. Watch for these clues to how they are feeling. Responding quickly will help them cry less.

PARENTS' SURVIVAL GUIDE

ADJUSTING TO PREMATURITY

All babies need a lot of help adjusting to the bright, noisy world outside the womb. Premature babies, who are born between three and 16 weeks early, need even more care to cope with this transition.

If you are one of the one in ten parents who had your baby sooner than the average 40 weeks, it will also help you to take things more slowly, so you don't feel overwhelmed. Your baby was born before they were ready to leave the womb, so their senses and nervous system are not as developed as a full-term baby's. They are also less likely to have the strength to communicate their needs as strongly, because their lungs are not yet strong enough to cry loudly – and the earlier your baby was born, the longer it will take for them to catch up. But remember that most premature babies reach the same development level as their full-term peers by the time they are between two and three years old.

1
Continue a womb-like feeling
A premature infant finds it harder to screen out sound and light, so the world can quickly feel too much. So, imagine the world from their perspective, and aim first to continue giving them the kind of calm, warmth, and dim lighting they had in the womb.

4
Offer white noise
Your baby may find it hard to sleep without either the low rumble they heard in the uterus or the machinery noises they heard in the premature baby unit. They may feel soothed by continuous white noise when you bring them home. This could be the whirr of a fan or a machine designed to replicate those sounds.

WORKING THINGS OUT
6 key principles

2
Try kangaroo care
Lay your baby skin to skin on your chest. Keep them warm under a front-fastening top, special wrap, or light blanket. They can then feel your or your co-parent's heartbeat, body warmth, and voice. As you do this, breathe deeply to help regulate yourself and your baby. As much as possible, put away your phone (make sure you don't fall asleep in a soft chair or a sofa, to avoid the risk of suffocation).

3
Let go of expectations
Premature babies need to be fed more and can be harder to settle. Let go of any expectations about "routines" and focus on meeting your baby's needs in the moment. Take advice from medical professionals who know your baby's history. If people comment on your baby's smaller size or development, respond by saying your baby is busy catching up after being born early.

5
Appreciate what you've been through
Both you and your baby have been taken by surprise. If you've seen your baby surrounded by machines and monitors, it's likely to have triggered shock and stress. Give yourself compassion and expect ups and downs after you come home from hospital. It might take a few weeks for your high levels of stress to start to fall. Allow time to settle and feel safe again once your baby is home.

6
Accept counselling
As your baby starts to catch up and grow, they will thrive most with a happy, confident, connected parent who can meet their emotional needs. Make the most of any counselling services on offer at your baby's birth unit, so you can express any unprocessed trauma from the birth and the weeks afterwards in a safe space with someone who understands.

TAILORED ADVICE

Sing and talk
While your baby may not be able to interact much yet, sing and talk to them. They already love listening to you, and this will help them grow and thrive.

Offer daily massage
Now your baby is home, they are ready to enjoy your touch. Premature babies are often stressed from medical interventions. Massage has been found to boost the growth and immune systems of pre-term infants.

Spend time with older children
If you have other children, they may feel confused and abandoned by your absence amid the drama of the new arrival. Ask for support from friends and family so you can find a daily window for reassuring one-on-one time with them. Point out how your preemie baby responds to their older brother or sister's presence.

"WHY DOES MY BABY STARTLE SO EASILY?"

Human babies come into the world relatively helpless. But they also arrive with a set of automatic reflexes, wired into their brains by evolution, which may take you, and them, by surprise.

SCENARIO | When you put your baby down, they fling their arms open and arch their back before letting out a cry and bringing their arms together.

Babies sometimes startle and freeze when they hear loud noises or are surprised by bright lights. Although it may seem to come out of the blue, there are two reasons. One is that if a newborn's head falls below the level of their body, they sense this change in position in the semi-circular canals in their ears, making them feel like they are falling. This triggers the Moro Reflex, dating back millions of years to when our ancestors lived in trees and infants clung on to their mothers by their fur. This is your baby's ancient instinct to find you and hold on tight.

The other reason your baby may appear to jump out of their skin is the Startle Reflex, triggered by loud noises, or changes of temperature or light. At these moments, they may freeze, blink, and their heart rate will go up. This is an early sign of your baby's developing fight-or-flight response.

WHAT YOU MIGHT BE THINKING

Why is my baby so jumpy?
They seem to jump out of their skin for no reason.

WHAT THEY MIGHT BE THINKING

◉ **As your baby grows in utero**, they get used to being held in a tight space. So being out in the world with nothing around them can make them feel unsupported and unsafe.

◉ **Newborns experience the world** through their bodies, so reaching out for your touch or for the security of something solid is one of the main ways of exploring the space around them.

◉ **Your baby can panic** if they feel exposed when they are moving through space without feeling you close to them.

◉ **After about two months**, the Moro Reflex will start to fade as your baby's neck muscles get stronger and they can hold their heads up. They will hold onto the Startle Reflex through life to protect them from sudden movements.

HOW YOU COULD RESPOND

In the moment

Lay them down with care
As you put your baby down, in a bath for example, lay them bottom first and support their heads, as horizontally as possible.

Stay close
As you lay them down in a cot, bend over to keep your body close and let go only when their whole body is in contact with the mattress.

Try swaddling
Swaddling in a light breathable blanket from birth can help give your baby the same feeling of safety as they did in the womb.

In the long term

Carry them in a sling
When they are newborn, your baby will feel most secure when they stay close to you. Try carrying them in a sling around your home, as well as when you go outside, to give them the security of feeling in close contact.

Give floor time
You baby is now learning how their body moves in space. When they are feeling alert and playful, give them time on the floor to get used to the freedom of moving their limbs in an open environment, and strengthen their muscles and motor skills.

Keep an eye out
If your baby only throws out their limbs on one side or the Moro Reflex doesn't disappear by six months old – or their Startle Reflex seems extreme – chat to your baby's health professional.

SEE RELATED TOPICS
Why does my baby grip so hard?: pp.44-45

> **" "**
> THE MORO REFLEX IS YOUR BABY'S ANCIENT INSTINCT TO FIND YOU AND HOLD TIGHT.

"HOW DOES MY BABY KNOW HOW TO FEED?"

Your baby may look helpless when they are born, but they have an innate instinct to seek out milk, and are wired with reflexes they need to feed – and the ability to tell you when they are hungry or full.

SCENARIO | Even though you are not yet sure how to feed them, your baby seems to have the instincts they need to find a nipple or teat to feed from.

While your baby doesn't yet have full control of their movements, if you brush their cheek or corner of their mouth, this triggers a reflex – wired into their primal lower brain – that makes them turn their head towards the sensation. This "rooting reflex" means they will then open their mouth and thrust out their tongue to search for milk.

As soon as they feel a nipple or teat brushing the roof of their mouths, a second reflex will kick in. This is the "sucking reflex", which triggers them to repeatedly press their tongue up to squeeze milk directly to the back of the mouth. To complete the process, babies come with a "swallowing reflex", the ability to close the top of the windpipe as they swallow, so they don't choke. By four months, the first two reflexes disappear.

WHAT YOU MIGHT BE THINKING

My baby seems to know more about this than I do!
I really want to know the signs that they are hungry or full, so I know I am feeding them enough.

WHAT THEY MIGHT BE THINKING

• **In the womb**, your baby practised feeding by swallowing 200–450 ml (7¼–15¾fl oz) of amniotic fluid every day by the time they were born. This made up around 10 per cent of their nutritional needs.

• **Your baby has been practising** how to suck while in the womb. Scans show embryos starting to suck their hands as soon as five months after conception.

• **Your newborn is drawn to the sweet smell of milk**. Infants develop a sense of taste in their last three months in the womb, thanks to the sweet flavour of the amniotic fluid. Milk also triggers the reward centres in their brain, because it is the most nutritious food source for them now.

• **Hunger triggers stress hormones**, like cortisol, which make your baby feel under threat. Feeding until they are satisfied will trigger feel-good chemicals in their bodies, like dopamine and oxytocin, which make them feel safe and connected to you.

HOW YOU COULD RESPOND

In the moment

Let them root
Rather than force a nipple or teat into their mouth, trigger the feeding reflex by gently brushing your finger, nipple, or bottle tip against their cheek to get them searching, latching on, and primed for feeding.

Don't leave it too late
If you miss early hunger cues your baby will panic to the point where they can't calm down enough to latch on. Look for signs before that such as sucking on their hands or your skin.

Trust their instincts
Be guided by your infant's reflexes. For example, the rooting reflex will help them find the best latching position.

Check their cues
By observing your baby carefully from the start, you will soon recognize signs that they are hungry – like rooting, clenched fists, and agitated movements of their legs and arms. You will also spot the cues that they have had enough, like turning away and unclenching their hands.

In the long term

Make it special time
Set up comfortable feeding stations around your home so that you can enjoy feeding times. Put away your phone so that you can stroke your baby, hold eye contact with one another, and spot the signals that they are full.

Be prepared
Your newborn's tummy is about the size of a hazelnut, expanding to the size of an egg by the time they are about a month old. At first, this means they will need 8–12 or even more feeds every 24 hours, but the gaps between feeds will gradually get longer. By the time they are two months old, they will need to be fed roughly every three to four hours, and by six months old, every four to five hours.

Expect night-time feeds
Your baby will be woken up during the night by hunger pangs – and this is when they get 20 per cent of their daily calorie needs.

SEE RELATED TOPICS
Why is my baby always hungry?: pp.42-43

"WHAT CAN MY BABY HEAR?"

For the last three months, your newborn has listened to your voice from the womb. Soon after they are born, they will recognize your voice when you speak.

SCENARIO | When you talk, your baby turns their head towards you and stares at you.

Your baby arrives in the world with a good sense of hearing, though it's not yet as sharp as it will be. They recognize your voice because their auditory system has been working well enough to hear from around week 25 in the womb. Even though your infant was surrounded by fluid that buffered sound, the sound of your voice got through.

While your baby may not be able to understand the words you use, they have been tuning into their pattern and cadence – and can even recognize the language and accent you speak in, as well as your emotional tone. As babies are born seeking connection to their parents for protection, they look to put a face to the voice they have heard.

WHAT YOU MIGHT BE THINKING

My baby sometimes stops to look at me when I talk. How do they recognize my voice so quickly?

SEE RELATED TOPICS
Why does my baby love to bang and clap?: pp.102-103

WHAT THEY MIGHT BE THINKING

- **Soon after birth**, your baby will look first for their birth mother's voice, closely followed by the voice of their co-parent if you've been together throughout the pregnancy. They will stop to listen to your voices when they are upset, and be soothed by them.

- **Your baby is so attuned** to the cadence of their mother's voice that researchers have discovered they subtly mimic these patterns in their cries. Within days they have been found to prefer their mother's voice to anyone else's.

- **From birth**, your baby will show a startle response to loud sudden noises, including their own cry. They may react to loud noises by going quiet or making a face.

- **If your infant heard the same tune** often when they were in the womb, like a song you listened to when you were pregnant, they may stop to listen to it now.

HOW YOU COULD RESPOND

In the moment

Start talking
Even though they don't yet understand what you say, talking to them helps build neural pathways in the parts of your baby's brain that process speech. To help develop their listening skills, chat to them and explain all the things you are seeing and doing.

Speak in "parentese"
Your baby will take most notice if you talk to them in a slow, high, repetitive sing-song voice that they can hear more easily. As the months go on, this style of talking will also help them break down the syllables of your language so they can start to mimic them.

Look at your baby as you speak
As they listen to you speak, your baby will also be looking at your mouth to see how you produce the sounds, so they can eventually do the same.

In the long term

Avoid loud noises
Your baby's inner ear is sensitive. As far as possible, steer clear of loud noises over 115 decibels, like heavy machinery, loud vehicle noise, and booming music. Keep noise to a level that you can talk over. Avoid arguing in front of your baby, as they can already tell the difference between different emotions. They will register aggression as stressful and frightening because they are so helpless.

Point out sounds
As they start to turn their heads in the direction of noises that interest them, point out different sounds such as birdsong or animal noises, so they make the link to where the sound is coming from.

Keep an eye out
If your baby doesn't startle at loud sudden noises, mention it to your health visitor or doctor so they can check if they need extra support with their hearing.

PARENTS' SURVIVAL GUIDE

CO-PARENTING

The greatest gift you can give your baby is not the most high-end pram or the most expensive nursery. It's caregivers who are happy, on the same team, and who give them a sense that the world is a safe place.

This will also give you more emotional bandwidth to connect with your child, read their cues, and meet their needs. If you are raising your child with a co-parent, it's also important to nurture and meet the needs of your relationship so you have a secure foundation on which to do this. Don't feel guilty about putting yourselves first at times in order to create a more stable environment for your child. View the upheaval of the first few months as a phase that will pass once your child becomes used to their new life in your family.

1
Face the challenge together
Becoming parents will shake up your relationship. As you will be doing a lot of relay parenting to start with, fix a daily time to reconnect, even if it's just ten minutes, and make it criticism-free.

4
Let go of perfectionism
Parents tend to worry more these days about getting "parenting" right. Avoid allowing one person to become the "expert" on your baby and embrace your differences and strengths as parents. Accept you are both learning and will both make mistakes along the way. Even if you put a nappy on your baby backwards, it's not life-threatening.

Co-parenting 41

WORKING THINGS OUT
8 key principles

2
Move beyond gender roles
If you both can, make the most of parental leave on offer. Time dads spend with babies changes their brain chemistry and makes them more bonded fathers. Fathers can also experience post-partum depression and anxiety.

3
Swap roles
Your baby will benefit from having co-parents who can swap roles. From the start, set out to share basic tasks like nappy changing. Work to your strengths and capabilities.

5
Find different ways to feel close
Sleepless nights and feeding mean you may lose the physical intimacy you once had as a couple. Until you recalibrate, look for other ways to feel physically close. These could be smaller sensual gestures that don't have to end in intercourse; a passionate kiss or loving texts.

6
Talk about money
Having a baby is likely to alter your financial dynamics. One partner may be giving up work, and feel less financially powerful, while the other may feel they have to work harder to provide, leaving their co-parent feeling abandoned. Discuss how you will budget now, so you are on the same page.

7
Ask for help
For millennia, children were brought up by a community of family members, not just one or two parents working around the clock. Don't try and do it alone. Invite trusted and willing family members and friends to be part of your baby's "village".

8
Be self-aware
You may find you have strong ideas about the "right" and "wrong" ways to care for your baby. Question where these ideas come from. Pick a calm time to talk and use sentences starting with "I feel". If you feel upset, ask yourself what lies beneath it – and be prepared to share this vulnerability.

TAILORED ADVICE

Seek counselling if needed
Young babies who see arguments between their parents can feel it as a threat to their survival. If it happens regularly and they are not soothed and comforted, they can grow into children who feel unsafe even when the initial stressor has passed. If your relationship is struggling, view seeking counselling as a commitment to the future mental health of your child.

Think about your shared goals
If you are no longer in a romantic relationship with your co-parent, remember you both want the same thing for your children: for them to grow into emotionally healthy, independent adults. Frame this as a joint goal you are both working towards.

"WHY IS MY BABY ALWAYS HUNGRY?"

In their first month, your baby is growing fast, gaining about 28g (1oz) every day – and it's all powered by milk. As they need so much to grow, it may feel like you're constantly feeding them.

SCENARIO | Your new baby wants to be fed all the time, sometimes for periods of up to an hour.

Your newborn's stomach can hold around a teaspoon of milk. As your baby grows, they will also need 100 calories per kg (2lb) of their body weight every day. As human milk is designed to be easy for an infant to digest, it moves quickly through the stomach and intestines, in as little as 1.5 to 2 hours. Formula takes about four hours. This means that your baby is often getting messages from their body that they need more fuel. Even though, at first, it might seem like they are hungry all the time, your baby will settle down into a more regular schedule of bigger feeds, with longer intervals.

WHAT YOU MIGHT BE THINKING

All I seem to do is feed my baby. It's exhausting. Are they getting enough milk, as they always seem hungry?

SEE RELATED TOPICS
When will my baby stop crying?: pp.52-53

WHAT THEY MIGHT BE THINKING

◉ **Your baby's body signals that their stomach is empty.** This triggers stress hormones, which make them cry for help.

◉ **If their hunger signals are not met as soon as they would like,** they will quickly start to get more distressed (and become harder to soothe) because they can't survive unless you come to their aid.

◉ **Your baby will also feel hungrier during growth spurts,** The first one may be 7 to 10 days after they born when they start to gain weight after an initial dip.

◉ **When your baby is full,** they may seem more bright-eyed, awake, and eager to engage.

> **YOUR BABY WILL FEEL HUNGRIER DURING GROWTH SPURTS.**

HOW YOU COULD RESPOND

In the moment

Offer responsive feeding
To start with, feed as often as they want, until they settle into a more regular pattern. If you are breastfeeding on demand, feeding will help stimulate your mammary glands to produce the right amount for your baby.

Let them control the flow of formula milk
Hold your baby in a semi-upright position on your lap with the teat horizontal. This will give your baby a chance to slow down how much milk they take in and control the pace of feeding. If you lie your baby down and hold their bottle more vertically, it's hard for them to control the flow. They could take in too much, making them vomit.

Watch for your baby's hunger signals
They will start by wriggling, opening and closing their mouths, and rooting. Next, they may stretch or put their hands in their mouths. In the final stage, they will cry, their limbs will get agitated, and they become red-faced.

In the long term

Watch for cues they have had enough
Healthy, emotionally regulated babies will generally stop feeding when they have had enough. Clues include turning their head away, ignoring the bottle or the nipple, relaxing, and unclenching their hands.

Respond to your baby's tempo
Babies can take anywhere from 20 minutes to an hour when they feed.

Remember you're not doing "nothing"
If you're used to being busy at work, sitting still to feed your baby for long periods may make you feel like you're "doing nothing" all day. Instead, view breast or bottle feeding as an essential, albeit slower-paced, opportunity to get to know your baby.

"WHY DOES MY BABY GRIP SO HARD?"

Your newborn came into the world with the primitive reflex to hold on tight to you, both with their hands and their feet.

SCENARIO | When you put your finger into your baby's palm, they immediately grip it. You notice their toes curl when you brush the balls of their feet.

Your infant arrives with a set of inbuilt reflexes to help them stay close to you. Lasting for a few months after birth, one of these is the grasp – or palmar – reflex. If you put your finger in your baby's palm, they will automatically close their fingers (not yet their thumbs) around yours and keep gripping.

Similarly, if you press your forefinger against the ball of your baby's foot, they will instinctively curl their toes up, too. This ability to grab is so great that if you carefully dangle a baby from their hands, they are able to support their own weight, a feat most adults could not achieve.

WHAT YOU MIGHT BE THINKING

How does my baby know how to do this? It's so sweet, but it really hurts when they grab my hair and won't let go.

WHAT THEY MIGHT BE THINKING

- **At first** your baby will mainly hold their hands in a fist position, just as they held them in the womb where there was little space.

- **Your baby develops their reflex to grasp** as early as 16 weeks after conception. Foetuses can be seen grasping the umbilical cord in scans.

- **It doesn't matter** who puts their finger in your newborn's hand. It's a reflex they have no voluntary control over yet, so they will grasp anything.

- **Your newborn does not yet realize** they are a separate person to you. If they pull your hair, they will have no idea that it hurts, or understand why you react in pain.

SEE RELATED TOPICS
Why is my baby crawling like that?: pp.80-81

HOW YOU COULD RESPOND

In the moment

Look out for it
Not all palmar grasps are the same. Babies will grip harder before they are fed than after. Look out for it as a hunger cue.

Use it to help feeding
There is a close link between the palmar grasp and the sucking reflex. If your baby is having trouble latching on to a nipple or teat, gently massage their palms to stimulate them to open their mouth and start sucking.

Unlock their grip
If your baby makes a painful grab for your hair, unlock their grip by pressing gently on the back of their hand and bending it slightly forwards. This is a quick, painless way to get them to let go.

In the long term

Strengthen hands
You can help your baby develop stronger hand muscles by giving them daily tummy time. When you put them on their front, they will lean on their hands and then push up, an essential step for rolling and crawling.

Keep an eye out
Your baby's palmar grasp is tested at birth, and they will get regular checks. But if you notice it's not even on both sides, very weak, or lasts after six months, mention it to your doctor or health visitor.

Watch their progress
As your baby starts to lean on their hands more, they will no longer hold their hands in a fist all the time.

Offer textures
Your baby is developing their sense of touch from birth. Try placing different-textured toys in their palms.

> " "
> YOUR INFANT ARRIVES WITH A SET OF INBUILT REFLEXES TO HELP THEM STAY CLOSE TO YOU. ONE OF THESE IS THE GRASP – OR PALMAR – REFLEX.

"WHY DOES MY BABY STICK OUT THEIR TONGUE?"

Your baby came into the world ready to communicate with you and to copy you. One of the first ways they might do this is by sticking out their tongue to mimic you.

SCENARIO | As you look at your baby and pull faces at them, they stick their tongue out at you a few seconds after seeing you do it.

Your baby came into the world with a strong tongue thrust reflex, which helps them use this strong muscle to push up against your nipple, or the teat of a bottle, to push out milk – as well as to prevent choking. They also have proportionally large tongues for their mouths. So in their first few months you will see their tongue slip out more when they are hungry, they feel full, or when they don't like a taste.

However, while most of these movements are reflexive, it may be one of the first deliberate motor skills babies develop. If you stick your tongue out while looking at them, you may notice they deliberately mimic you as early as the first week after birth.

WHAT YOU MIGHT BE THINKING

Is that just a reflex when their tongue comes out, or could my baby really be trying to copy me?

WHAT THEY MIGHT BE THINKING

● **The tongue** is one of the first body parts your baby seems to have conscious control over. By seeing you stick your tongue out and doing the same with theirs, it's the first sign they understand they are a separate being with equivalent body parts.

● **When you smile** and stick your tongue back out in response, your baby feels the pleasure of pleasing you. This triggers the release of feel-good chemicals, encouraging them to do it again.

● **Your baby is learning** basic cause and effect: when they do something, something else happens in return. This could be their first "serve and return" social conversation, as well as their first "game".

● **By watching the movements** of your mouth intently, they are practising their lip-reading skills and observing how you make the sounds to produce words.

SEE RELATED TOPICS
Has my baby started smiling?: pp.62-63,
Why does my baby babble?: pp.72-73

HOW YOU COULD RESPOND

In the moment

Get the ball rolling
Choose a time when your baby is fed, alert, and interested and when there is not too much noise. As you face them, try sticking your tongue out and see what happens. Don't force it. Your baby will do it when they work out they have a tongue just like you and they have conscious control of it.

If they look away or start fussing, bring the game to an end.

Give them a moment
After you've stuck your tongue out for a few seconds, wait for a few seconds. It can take a few moments for your baby to observe what you are doing and then respond.

In the long term

Read the cues
They are many reasons babies stick out their tongues, so observe the context. They may do it to root for food when they are hungry or to push out food when they are full. For now, they will only be imitating you if they are also staring intently at you and have an interested expression in their eyes.

Keep an eye out
Most babies will grow out of the extrusion – or tongue thrust reflex – by around four months, and the gradual fading of this response is one of the signs they are getting ready to try solid foods. If their tongue thrust continues past six months and it's stopping them trying solids, mention it to your baby's health care team.

> ❝ ❞
>
> **THE TONGUE IS ONE OF THE FIRST BODY PARTS YOUR BABY HAS CONSCIOUS CONTROL OVER.**

CO-SLEEPING

What your new baby wants most is to be close to you. This helps them to feel safe, regulates their temperature and breathing, and brings down their stress levels.

It's for this reason that babies have slept with their immediate family throughout the evolution of mankind, and it's still done in many parts of the world today. As babies wake up as many as two or three times a night because of their smaller tummies and shorter sleep cycles – and panic when they don't feel you near – bringing your baby to bed can mean less interrupted sleep. Getting more rest may then help you bond, as well as feel happier and more engaged with your child during the day. However, before you decide to share your bed with your baby, it's important to think about how to make it as risk-free as possible.

1
Calculate the risk
If you or your partner smoked, drank, or took recreational drugs during your pregnancy, avoid co-sleeping. All raise the risk of Sudden Infant Cot Death before the age of one. Co-sleeping is also a higher risk for babies who were premature or who weighed under 2.5kg (5½lbs) at birth.

4
Design your sleep space
A safe co-sleeping space includes a firm mattress in good condition. Remove pillows that could fall on your baby, and swap duvets for lighter blankets. Think about a sleep sack for your baby. Fill any gaps (such as between mattress and bed frame) into which your infant could roll and suffocate. Tie back long hair, which can wrap around a baby's neck.

WORKING THINGS OUT

6 key principles

2
Agree with your co-parent
If co-sleeping feels right, agree the way forward together. Take shared responsibility for not drinking alcohol or taking drugs or medication that could make you sleep more heavily. Be flexible. If you and your partner are not sleeping well with your baby in your bed, work on soothing your child to sleep on their own. As long as there's lots of closeness and intimacy during the day, they should not miss out on bonding.

3
Consider how you feed
Breastfeeding can make co-sleeping safer than formula feeding. Research has found that mothers giving their own milk tend naturally to curl their bodies around their infants, who sleep at breast level. This forms a protective C shape around them.

5
Never sleep with your baby on the sofa
This has been found to increase the risk of sudden infant death by as much as 50 times, because of the risk of babies slipping between cushions or into gaps. Ask your partner to wake you if you fall asleep with your baby on the couch, and do the same for them. Avoid sleeping with your other children and pets, too. This also raises the risk for babies, because there is a higher chance of smothering.

6
Teach sleep skills
As they grow, teach your child the skill of falling asleep on their own. Between four to eight months, look for cues they are ready to do so, like becoming happier to spend a bit of time by themselves. Start by putting them in their own cot next to you, before moving them into their own bedroom. At night, use comfort objects that smell of you to remind them you are not far.

TAILORED ADVICE

Be intimate elsewhere
Many couples worry that co-sleeping will get in the way of closeness and resuming sex after birth. Think about ways to be intimate at other times or in other parts of your home so you maintain your intimacy.

There are many ways to co-sleep
The NHS in the UK recommends that babies sleep in a parent's bedroom for their first six months so you are there to comfort them and keep an eye on them during the night. This can take many forms, from a bassinet next to your bed, to a cot designed to attach to the side. This allows the baby to stay close but also have their own space which you can't roll onto.

"DOES MY BABY RECOGNIZE ME?"

Your baby was born able to recognize your smell and voice. As their vision and memory have got better they now know you are special to them, even if they also smile at people they don't know.

SCENARIO | When you go into a shop and a stranger smiles at your baby, they beam back in the same way they smile at you.

Your baby knows you the moment they come into the world by your voice, which they heard in utero – and by your smell, which they recognize from the amniotic fluid that surrounded them. As soon as they were born, they started scanning your face to memorize it and to connect with you. Studies show that babies recognize their main caregivers by the time they are two or three weeks old.

Every positive interaction you have with your baby deepens their attachment to you. Over time, they have learned you are the person they trust most to meet their needs and make them feel safe – and they will show this with smiles and laughter. However, your baby will also smile at new people, if you do, because you are showing it's safe to do so, and they have not developed a fear of strangers.

WHAT YOU MIGHT BE THINKING

My baby smiles at everyone and it's lovely. But I am wondering if they know I am special to them.

SEE RELATED TOPICS
What can my baby see?: pp.26-27

WHAT THEY MIGHT BE THINKING

● **Your baby is hardwired** from birth to be interested in human faces, and in new ones. Research shows that even newborns are confused if shown pictures of faces missing key features.

● **Even if they smile at others** from the safety of your arms, by around five weeks old, research has found that babies get tense if they are picked up by strangers.

● **Your baby won't start to miss you** until they've developed "object permanence" – understanding that people exist in the world even when you can't see them – between four and seven months old.

"Does my baby recognize me?"

> **BABIES RECOGNIZE THEIR MAIN CAREGIVERS BY THE TIME THEY ARE TWO OR THREE WEEKS OLD.**

HOW YOU COULD RESPOND

In the moment

Maximize eye contact
The more time you spend connecting with your baby visually from birth, with eye contact, the sooner they will recognize your face.

Smile
Your baby will recognize you sooner if you also smile and laugh with them. This shared experience will stimulate the emotion centres in their brains and build the attachment between you. And your baby is watching you to see how to respond to new people you meet, so if you smile at new people, they are likely to do the same.

Help them recognize you in other ways
When you are not in your baby's eyeline, chat or sing to them so they still have the security of knowing you are close by, even when they can't see you.

In the long term

Share the care
Your baby needs to see someone frequently to recognize them. By six months, they are likely to recognize a relative they have played with once a week. Head off separation anxiety further down the line by regularly sharing their care with other trusted people.

Make faces
Once the memory of your face is embedded, you can experiment with making funny faces. Because they remember how your face is "supposed" to look, your baby may find it funny when you look different, as long as you then return to your smiling expression.

Start peekaboo
If they are ready, try this game of hiding and revealing your face. It will also tell your baby you will always come back, even when they lose sight of you.

"WHEN WILL MY BABY STOP CRYING?"

When your baby is born, crying is the most attention-grabbing way they have to communicate their needs. With time and practice, you will work out what different cries mean.

SCENARIO | Your baby has been crying continuously for two hours and you can't work out what's wrong.

At first, all your newborn baby's cries may sound like general alarm calls. You may sometimes feel helpless, but there are ways to interpret what your infant is trying to say – and help them cry less.

Infants cry for these reasons: hunger, tiredness, overwhelm, loneliness, pain and discomfort, and boredom and frustration. All cries tend to sound the same at first, but as you tune in, you're likely to notice subtle differences in pitch and intensity. Combine context, like when they were last fed, with body language and facial expressions, and you will learn to translate what your baby is trying to say.

WHAT YOU MIGHT BE THINKING

I can't cope with them crying for this long. I can't tell what they want. It's so stressful.

WHAT THEY MIGHT BE THINKING

- **Until they develop other ways to communicate**, crying is your infant's emergency call to get your attention when their other cues have not been picked up. It's their way of saying, "I need you now. I can't wait any longer."

- **When your baby cries**, there are physiological changes in their nervous system. There is a rise in stress hormones like cortisol, and their breathing and heart rate.

- **Your baby relies on you** for survival. Once the threat detector in their brain, the amygdala, is triggered, the only way they know to calm themselves is by asking you to hold and soothe them.

- **Your baby doesn't have wants**, only needs. They can't manipulate or try to control you. Crying is the only way they have to express their fear that they can't get their needs met.

SEE RELATED TOPICS
Why does my baby babble?: pp.72-73

HOW YOU COULD RESPOND

In the moment

Spot hunger cries
If your baby is hungry, their cry will be more constant and rhythmic. It's louder than other cries, but lower pitched.

Spot tired cries
Tiredness triggers a rise in cortisol in infants, which can make it hard for them to settle. In this state, their cries are often accompanied by jerky arm and leg movements, rubbing their eyes, or clenching their fists.

Spot overwhelmed cries
When your baby is exposed to too much bright light, noise, or new sensations, they will cry and also look away or try to nuzzle into you to block out the outside world.

Spot distressed or pain cries
Studies have found that when babies are in pain their cries are more erratic and higher pitched. They breathe faster with fewer pauses. They may also arch their backs.

Spot bored cries
They may start to make on-and-off cries and kick their legs more to get your attention. If that doesn't work, this fussiness will develop into a low, constant cry.

Offer skin to skin contact
Research has found that putting your newborn against your bare skin will help them regulate more quickly. Placing your baby in a sling may also meet their need to be close, and reduce crying, according to research.

Stick with it
If your baby is overwhelmed, it can take time for them to regulate. Research has found that walking a baby up and down for five minutes, then sitting and holding them for a further five to eight minutes, works best to help calm crying babies to sleep.

In the long term

Be an observer
Research shows that parents go through a learning curve about understanding their child's cries. Trust you will learn with experience. Babies who are consistently comforted in their early months are generally less stressed, more confident, and less anxious in their relationships.

Reframe your response
If you are tired and trying to do too much alone, it's easy to hear crying as an accusation from your baby that you are doing something wrong. Instead, view crying instead as your child's earliest attempts to communicate with you until they develop more skills.

See it as a phase
There is a peak in crying between three and six weeks, when the average baby will cry between one and two hours a day, often more in the late afternoon and evening, perhaps due to a build-up of overstimulation and tiredness.

Don't compare
Some babies come into the world with naturally more sensitive temperaments, which are harder to soothe. Avoid comparisons with other infants and reassure yourself that as long as you are responsive most of the time, you are giving your child what they need.

Look for the bigger picture
At times your baby will cry for no understandable reason. Remember that it's not crying that harms your baby, it's being left alone with their distress. However, if your baby is often crying for long periods for none of the more common reasons, mention it to your doctor or health visitor so they can rule out any illness or pain.

"CAN MY BABY TELL NIGHT FROM DAY?"

One of the biggest challenges for new parents is that babies are born not yet knowing the difference between night and day.

SCENARIO | Your baby seems to be just as alert when they wake up during the night as they do during the day, leaving you feeling exhausted.

In the womb, it's always dark. The light hitting the back of our eyes is what governs our body clocks – or circadian rhythm – so it's understandable that at birth, babies can't tell night from day.

At first, newborns sleep about 70 per cent of the time. They are awake as much in the night as the day. They gradually shift towards sleeping more when it's dark; it won't be until at least two months that their brain starts to register all the signals from the environment and their bodies that it's time for sleep. By six to nine months, most infants have adapted enough to sleep at least six hours at night.

WHAT YOU MIGHT BE THINKING

When does this end? Getting up in the middle of the night is leaving me tired and irritable. Sometimes my baby is awake for ages, and I feel alone trying to cope.

WHAT THEY MIGHT BE THINKING

- **Your newborn is more active at night** because they are still on uterine time. When you walked around during the day when you were pregnant, this tended to rock your unborn baby to sleep. When you stopped at bedtime, this woke them up, so they tended to get more active. Now they are out in the world, they are still doing the same.

- **Your baby has a small stomach.** When it's empty they may wake up, whatever time it is.

- **Your new baby moves in and out of sleep** more easily than you do. Their average sleep cycle lasts 20 to 50 minutes, compared to an adult cycle of 90 to 110 minutes. Babies are more likely to wake up in between cycles.

SEE RELATED TOPICS
What can my baby see?: pp.26-27

"IN THE WOMB, IT'S ALWAYS DARK, SO AT BIRTH, BABIES CAN'T TELL NIGHT FROM DAY.

HOW YOU COULD RESPOND

In the moment

Remember it's a phase
When it feels like you are the only person awake in the middle of the night, remember there are a lot of other parents doing the same. Try to enjoy the intimacy and connection you have with your baby in the small hours.

Keep phones away
Avoid having phone screens near your baby's face because the blue light may confuse them into thinking it's daylight. Babies are highly sensitive to this glow, which suppresses the production of melatonin, a hormone that tells the body it's time to sleep.

Make night-time a quiet time
When they wake up during the night, avoid stimulating your baby too much. Talk more quietly, and keep the lights dimmed, so your baby knows it's not time to play.

In the long term

See natural light
Light is the main way your baby will regulate their body clock. When it hits the back of the eye, the brain uses this information to time the release of sleep and wakefulness hormones. Walks before their first nap in the morning and in the early afternoon have been found to help babies set their body clock to be ready to sleep at night.

Make day and night different
Changing light levels will help your baby develop their internal body clock. Make the room they sleep in dark and open the curtains in the morning to let in sunlight.

Give different cues
To help your baby understand the difference between daytime naps and night-time sleep, create different routines. For instance, during the day, sing a lullaby and put them in a Moses basket next to you. At night, give different cues and put them in their cot in the bedroom.

Introduce more regular mealtimes
Research has found that regular feeding times help babies develop circadian rhythms.

PARENTS' SURVIVAL GUIDE

BABIES AND **SLEEP**

Sleep looms large among parents' biggest concerns during their child's early years. Some of that is due to anxiety from cultural messages about when babies "should" start sleeping through the night.

However, if you see sleep from the point of view of your baby's development, you will feel more empowered. Your newborn will sleep for around 17 hours a day because they need this rest to process their new experiences. It will take the first few months for their body clock to come "online" and release the hormones of wakefulness and sleepiness, which tie in with your adult sleep schedule. Working with your baby's biology – rather than trying to stick to strict rules – will make the transition to sleeping through the night easier.

1
Expect night-time waking
It is normal for newborns to wake up three to six times a night; they have short sleep cycles, small tummies, and soil their nappies often. Consider keeping your baby in your bedroom for the first six months, so it's easier for you to respond.

4
Don't let them "cry it out"
When your baby wakes up and cries, and you don't come, they may eventually give up calling for you because they are exhausted. If this happens regularly – before they are old enough to remember that you always come back – it can have a toxic effect on their developing brain. This includes the way their brain responds to stress, which can be hard to rewire later.

WORKING THINGS OUT

6 key principles

2
Avoid comparison
It will take a few months for your baby's body and brain to get on "adult time". With your support, your child will find their schedule. Having unrealistic expectations – and feeling anxious as a result – will be felt by your child, making learning to sleep through the night more drawn out.

3
Let them hear your heartbeat
The sound of your heartbeat is soothing to your baby because they were so used to hearing it in the womb. Hearing it after birth has been found to help them fall asleep more easily. If they are having trouble settling, try letting them lie skin-to-skin on your chest so they can listen to it.

5
Help them trust you are there
Avoid sleep training before six months. After this age, they know you are close by, even if they can't see you. Help them learn to fall asleep on their own by offering a transitional object – like a piece of cloth which smells of you – to help calm them. Or play a recording of your voice, which has been found to reduce the stress chemicals that help keep babies awake.

6
Observe sleep cues
If your baby is overtired, this can give them another burst of energy; fatigue triggers a spike in the wakefulness hormones cortisol and adrenaline. From birth, observe your child for subtle signs. These can include their bodies becoming more clenched, moving jerkily, looking away from you, grizzling, not wanting to look at toys, and having a glazed look. They may also try to block out light, and squirm.

> **SLEEP LOOMS LARGE AMONG PARENTS' CONCERNS DURING THE EARLY YEARS.**

TAILORED ADVICE

Create a bedtime routine
Every evening, get into the routine of doing things to dial down the levels of their alertness hormone cortisol and increase sleepiness hormones, like melatonin. This could include giving them a bath, followed by a massage, a cuddle, and finally, a story. You can also raise levels of melatonin by gradually dimming the lights in the run-up to bedtime.

Expect changes to their sleep
Changes to routine, teething, or learning new motor skills can all affect a baby's sleep and they may go back to needing you there to help them fall asleep. Stick to your usual routine and they should soon switch back to their normal bedtime behaviour.

Create your baby's sleep kit
Experiment with the kinds of lights, noises, and coverings your infant likes. Some prefer darkness and quiet, others soothing music. Some babies like to be wrapped up tight with heavy blankets, others prefer lighter covering.

"WHAT IS MY BABY STARING AT?"

At birth, your baby could only see for short distances. Development in their eyes, as well as more control and strength in their necks, means that by three to four months old they are now ready to turn their heads to look at things further away.

SCENARIO | When you go out for walks, your baby is now turning to look at more things in the world around them, like dogs in the park.

When your baby was born, their vision was the least developed of their five senses, partly because there was so little to see in the womb. They could only see clearly for 20–30cm (8–12in) and most objects looked like grey blurry shapes. Since then, the muscles that focus their eyes have grown stronger with use. This means they see with more sharpness and several feet into the distance. The view is more interesting too: at the back of their eyes, there is now a greater concentration of photoreceptors, including colour-sensitive cones. This means everything looks more colourful to your baby.

WHAT YOU MIGHT BE THINKING

My baby seems to be looking around and noticing things more. How much are they taking in? Do I need to give them lots of new things to look at?

WHAT THEY MIGHT BE THINKING

• **A newborn lays their head** to the side because their neck muscles are weak. Now, with more neck strength, they also move their heads to look straight ahead.

• **Your baby is now able to track objects** more easily and can smoothly follow the path of a moving object, like an animal or a ball rolling away.

• **Your baby may get "stuck"** looking at things because their developing vision now allows their gaze to focus more intensely. However, as this is still a new skill, their eyes can get locked on an object for several minutes.

• **Your baby loves novelty**. They will stare for around 30 seconds at something they have never seen.

SEE RELATED TOPICS
What can my baby see?: pp.26-27,
Does my baby recognize me?: pp.50-51

HOW YOU COULD RESPOND

In the moment

Keep it interesting
Your baby's brain is wired to be attracted by new things, particularly people and animals who are moving, so make plenty of trips outside to see new things. See where your baby is looking and name the objects for them.

Put objects just out of reach
Your baby is gradually getting better at working out how far away an object is. During tummy time, place things just out of reach to help them develop depth perception.

Give them something to swipe
Help your baby practise hand–eye coordination by placing objects just above them in a baby gym, so they can eventually reach for things they see.

In the long term

Roll things
Rolling moving objects like balls or wheeled cars will help your baby to learn to coordinate their eyes and use their eye muscles.

Use a rattle
Shaking a rattle on both sides of your baby will help infants practise turning their heads to look where a noise is coming from.

Watch for cross-eyes
If your baby seems to squint or their eyes still look "crossed" most of the time, or are not working together in a coordinated way, by the age of about six months, ask your GP for an extra eye examination.

" "

EVERYTHING LOOKS MORE COLOURFUL TO YOUR BABY.

"CAN MY BABY RECOGNIZE THEIR OWN NAME?"

You thought hard about what to call your baby, but it will take many months before they understand that their name is a special label that belongs just to them.

SCENARIO | You've chosen a name and bought personalized toys with it written on, then wonder how long it will be before your baby knows their name.

Your baby comes into the world primed to learn human language. In the womb, they learned to recognize your voice. After birth, they continue to listen to you all the time and watch your lips to see how you make the sounds. It will take many steps before they begin to make sense of the noises they hear when you speak to them. Even though their own name is one of the most common words they hear, by putting special emphasis on it, and looking at them each time you repeat it, their name could be the first word your baby recognizes, from about four to six months.

WHAT YOU MIGHT BE THINKING

I think my baby is turning to look at me when I say their name. Do they know what their name is yet?

▼ **SEE RELATED TOPICS**
What words can my baby understand?: pp.82–83

WHAT THEY MIGHT BE THINKING

◉ **Your baby is not aware** they are a separate person when they are first born. So they won't know they need a name to tell them apart from others.

◉ **Your infant will start** to pick up that their name means something special if you say it in a special song-song way, known as "parentese".

◉ **Gradually your baby will become aware** that you are likely to be looking and smiling at them when you say this special word, so it must mean something.

◉ **You will know** your baby is getting a grasp of what names are for when you refer to a sibling, pet, or caregiver by name and your infant looks in their direction.

> **THEIR NAME COULD BE THE FIRST WORD YOUR BABY RECOGNIZES, FROM ABOUT FOUR TO SIX MONTHS.**

HOW YOU COULD RESPOND

In the moment

Start sentences with their name
When you want to get your baby's attention, say their name, then pause to look at them before you speak. You could also ask them questions, for example: "Lily, is it time to change your nappy?"

Look at them as you say it
Have regular one-on-one time when they are alert, wide-eyed, and engaged, with no background noise. Say their name slowly and meaningfully, letting them watch you move your mouth so they can work out how you say it. Research has found that the more caregivers use eye contact with babies when they speak to them, the better babies get at identifying words from the stream of speech that they hear.

Keep using it
Repetition is the key to your child knowing their name. Try to avoid referring to your child just as "the baby" or "he" or "she", so they can hear their name repeated more often.

In the long term

Help them develop their sense of self
Make up a song about them and what they love to do to help them develop their sense of individuality and self. Music will also help them pick up the cadence of their name.

Play a name game
Your child is more likely to understand they have a name too if you show them how everyone in the family has one – including Mummy and Daddy. Refer to siblings and pets and caregivers and then point to them. Show them pictures of themselves and other people in photographs and point out their names, so they understand everyone has their own "label".

Be patient
Even if they can recognize their name between four and six months, it will still be many more months before they actually say their own name. It won't be until about 18 months to two years old that they talk about themselves as separate people.

"HAS MY BABY STARTED SMILING?"

Your baby wants to connect with you from the moment they come out of the womb. At first, the main way they do this is by gazing at your face. As they start to be able to copy your facial expressions, you will be rewarded with your first social smile.

SCENARIO | While holding your baby up to chat in "baby talk", you notice them slowly forming what looks like a smile.

Your baby started smiling in utero, as practice for the expressions they would need to communicate both fear and happiness after birth. However, for the first weeks, most of the smiles that pop up – when they are asleep, or burping – are reflexes, or a response to pleasant sensations, such as sweet tastes and smells.

By around six to 12 weeks, your baby has got better at coordinating the muscles in their face. This means they can make more recognizable smiling expressions. When you smile back, it makes them want to copy you, setting up a game of "serve and return." They also start to associate smiling with feeling good, setting up a positive feedback loop in their brain's reward system.

WHAT YOU MIGHT BE THINKING

I can't wait! Is this finally a real, deliberate smile – or the same as the expression they make when they're asleep or filling their nappy?

"Has my baby started smiling?" 63

WHAT THEY MIGHT BE THINKING

- **From the moment they are born**, your baby is fascinated by your face and wants to copy your expressions. They won't just copy your happy face either. If you observe carefully, you may notice they will also copy angry or sad expressions too.

- **When your baby** gives you a real social smile, you will be able to tell it apart from a reflexive smile, because they will be looking at you, and their face will light up, including their eyes. These "proper" smiles also last longer.

- **Your baby soon realizes** that when they smile, they hold your attention for longer. This makes them want to keep on doing it.

- **Your baby's smiling gets easier** with practise as they strengthen and learn to coordinate the 12 muscles they need to make this expression. Over the next few weeks, their smiles will become quicker and more symmetrical.

HOW YOU COULD RESPOND

In the moment

Keep smiling
Research shows that smiling at your baby as you hold their gaze and mirroring their expression helps build a secure, trusting attachment.

Pay attention
Babies learn to try and attract attention with your smiles. If babies don't get a response, they will smile less. So even if you're not yet sure whether it's a "social smile", take the chance to interact and smile at your baby anyway, so they know they are important to you.

Give them time
Babies react more slowly to smiles. It takes them several seconds. So hold their gaze when you smile, and give them plenty of time to respond.

In the long term

Don't overdo it
Your baby will smile most when they are feeling alert and content. If you try too hard or too long to make your baby smile, they can feel overwhelmed. If they start to look away, or become unsettled, give them a break. Avoid taking it personally or getting stressed about how often they smile, as your baby will pick up on your anxiety.

Keep an eye
If your baby hasn't smiled by around four months old, but is responsive when you speak to them, they may be just taking a little longer. Babies also show happiness by waving their limbs and squealing, so pay attention to these signs too. If your child is not interacting with you at all by this age, mention it to your baby's health professional.

SEE RELATED TOPICS
Why does my baby find that funny?: pp.90-91

" "

THEY ASSOCIATE SMILING WITH FEELING GOOD, SETTING UP A POSITIVE FEEDBACK LOOP.

"WHY DOES MY BABY TRY TO ROLL OVER?"

When your baby was born, they couldn't move from the spot where you put them down. As their core strength starts to develop between three and six months they will start rolling over, the first sign they are on the move.

SCENARIO | After putting your baby in the middle of your bed, you turn around to see they have rolled to the edge.

When your baby is born, their head is a quarter of their body weight and they lack the strength to lift it off the ground. At the same time, they are building the muscles in their trunk from kicking and reaching. When their core and neck strength start to combine, they are ready to make their first roll.

At first, your baby will probably tip over by accident when they turn their head. Although it may take them by surprise, your baby will discover they enjoy the freedom of being able to roll by themselves. They will then start practising and will intentionally shift their weight to roll both ways.

WHAT YOU MIGHT BE THINKING

My baby used to stay where I left them. Now when I look around, they are somewhere else. I need to think about where it's safe to put them now.

SEE RELATED TOPICS
Why does my baby love to be held in the air?: pp.74-75

WHAT THEY MIGHT BE THINKING

● **Your baby probably** didn't like being on their front at first. But with more arm strength they can push their chest up and then roll over, giving them more to look at.

● **Even though their first roll** took them off guard, your baby will start being delighted by the sensation and enjoy seeing the room from a different viewpoint.

● **At first when they roll**, your baby's arms and legs will get in the way. But within a few days they will work out how to use their limbs to push off and roll over.

● **Some babies will use rolling** as a way to get moving, until they have mastered crawling forward, which they will discover is a more efficient way to get around.

"Why does my baby try to roll over?"

HOW YOU COULD RESPOND

In the moment

Think where you leave your baby
Your baby will be pleased with their newfound skill but have no idea of the risks of falling.

Limit the use of restrictive baby equipment
Rather than keep them in enclosed baby equipment, give your baby plenty of time to discover what they can do with their body with free play on the floor.

Get the balance right
So they grow equally strong on their right and left, encourage your baby to roll their weight both ways by showing them interesting toys on both sides. Your baby will find it easier to learn to crawl if they have balanced strength.

In the long term

Encourage their technique
When they are lying on their tummy and ready to play, you could gently rock their bottom from side to side and cross one leg over the other to help them turn and roll.

Build up core muscles
If your baby is showing no sign of rolling, offer extra tummy time. If they don't like it alone on the floor, get down with them, face to face. You could also put a rolled towel under their chest to encourage them to raise their front, making rolling more likely. Just a few minutes several times a day will build your baby's strength.

Think about nappy changes
Now your baby has discovered the fun of rolling over, they may also try it during nappy changes. Use an anti-roll change mat which has slopes at the sides, to stop them falling off. Never leave them unattended.

> YOUR BABY WILL START BEING DELIGHTED BY THE SENSATION AND ENJOY SEEING THE ROOM FROM A DIFFERENT VIEWPOINT.

TOUCH

When they emerge into the world, touch is your baby's most developed sense. Cuddling your newborn is the best way you can give them the feeling of safety and security of being in the womb.

Touching their skin – the largest organ in the body – is also a key way for you to communicate, comfort, and bond with them. Think of stroking, rocking, and bathing your baby as the first language they understand. Allow yourself to enjoy it – and not be worried that your baby is somehow "breakable". Knowing that touch boosts your baby's emotional development can make holding your baby even more rewarding, especially as research shows that it's good for you, too.

1
Stroke your baby bump
Researchers have found that babies are more likely to touch the wall of the womb when their mother strokes her bump, probably because they are familiar with the pressure of their caress.

4
Be responsive
Babies respond to touch differently and develop preferences for different types of pressure and movement. Observe your baby for clues they are enjoying it or have had too much, like fussing or frowning.

> **TOUCHING IS A KEY WAY FOR YOU TO COMMUNICATE, COMFORT, AND BOND.**

WORKING THINGS OUT
8 key principles

2
Let touch bond you
Skin-to-skin contact between you and your newborn after birth has been found to boost interaction between parents and babies as long as a year later. It releases bonding oxytocin in you and your baby, making you feel closer.

3
Use skin-to-skin contact
Newborn babies find it hard to regulate their temperature. Holding them skin-to-skin on your chest will help them match yours, as well as your heartbeat and breathing rate. This also helps colonize your baby's skin with good bacteria.

5
Introduce massage
From birth, use massage to calm and regulate your baby. Lie your baby on your tummy face down and gently stroke their shoulders, back, arms, and legs for about a minute each if they are enjoying it. Make it multisensory by talking softly, humming, or singing.

6
Touch your baby to regulate them
Regular loving touch and massage help train your baby's nervous system to regulate itself, a lifelong asset for wellbeing. Gentle touch sends a message to the vagus nerve, the main superhighway for nerve impulses in your child's spine, which helps control the release of stress and relaxation hormones throughout the body.

7
Massage for pain relief
Studies have found that babies with colic who were massaged twice a day for 15–20 minutes cried less and slept more easily. Massage before and after has also been found to relieve pain when babies need vaccinations and heel-prick tests.

8
Helps premature babies thrive
In studies, premature babies who were touched regularly have been found to gain more weight than those who were not. They were also released from hospital five days earlier. It also reduces stress and pain, while massage has been found to help reduce the risk of infection.

TAILORED ADVICE

It's good for you too
Parents who give babies regular massages have less anxiety, and strong bonds with their babies. It also helps you build your confidence handling them and responding to their cues.

Share touch equally
Fathers who massage their babies every day have been found to be more expressive and show more enjoyment and warmth during interaction with their infants.

Develop children's own sense of touch
Give them different textures to try, like satin or cotton, or stroke them on the cheek. As they grow, introduce feeling words like "rough" and "smooth".

CHAPTER 2

YOUR 6–12 MONTH-OLD

"WHY DOES MY BABY SUCK ON EVERYTHING?"

Your baby's mouth is packed with nerve endings and taste buds – so sucking, tasting, chewing, and biting are some of the main ways they explore the world and learn about texture, taste, shape, and size.

SCENARIO | Your baby puts everything from the car keys to the TV remote control in their mouth.

Your baby is now developing a pincer grasp and coordination in their hands. They will start using these skills to bring objects to their mouths to explore them. They find this easy and satisfying because they have extra nerve endings in this area so they can feel for a nipple or teat for feeding.

Mouthing also helps your baby practise skills for eating solids, strengthening the jaw, cheek, and tongue muscles. You may sometimes be alarmed by the strange – and even dirty – things they want to suck on, but it also exposes them to microbes that can help build their immune systems.

WHAT YOU MIGHT BE THINKING

Yuck, they put horrible dirty things in their mouth. I am worried they are going to get sick. I say "No," but they do it anyway.

SEE RELATED TOPICS
What does the world feel like to my baby?: pp.28–29

WHAT THEY MIGHT BE THINKING

- **Even in the womb** your baby sucked their fingers to self-soothe. When they suck objects now, they still find it comforting.

- **Before your baby starts to get on the move**, mouthing is the easiest and most satisfying way to explore and understand the texture and shape of objects they come across.

- **Your baby doesn't know what's edible** and what's not, so they will taste everything. They are likely to spit out objects that taste bitter or unpleasant.

- **When they start teething** at around seven months old, chewing and biting on their gums relieves the pressure and distracts from the discomfort.

"My baby puts anything in their mouth!"

"
YOUR BABY'S MOUTH IS PACKED WITH NERVE ENDINGS AND TASTE BUDS.

HOW YOU COULD RESPOND

In the moment

Keep it playful
Rather than stress your baby by telling them off, try to create a "clean enough", safe space in your home where anything they come across is safe to put in their mouth.

Make a distinction
Although you don't want to discourage exploration, it may help to draw a simple line between things that are meant to go in their mouths, like food, and objects that aren't. If your baby puts a household object in their mouth you could say, "You can taste it but that's not for eating" or, "It isn't food." Intervene only when necessary, so they don't feel shamed or told off for being curious.

Create a distraction
If you see your child put something dirty or unsafe in their mouths, redirect them. For example, if you see them sucking on your keys, distract them with something else.

In the long term

Offer lots of textures
As well as their usual toys, offer them other safe objects with different weights, textures, and surfaces, such as spoons or toothbrushes.

Remove risky objects
So your baby can explore, scan your home for things that could be a swallowing, choking, or poisoning hazard. Look out for batteries, coins, and laundry capsules, as well as string, rubber bands, cat litter, and small hard food such as grapes.

Keep food to a dining area
If you give your baby food all over your home, it will be harder for them to distinguish between objects they can mouth, and food they can eat. Try to feed them mainly in the eating areas of your home.

"WHY DOES MY BABY BABBLE?"

Making words and learning to talk is as challenging for your baby as learning to walk. Babbling is the start of your child experimenting – and playing – with the kinds of sounds they can make.

SCENARIO | Your baby has gone from cooing and squealing to blowing loud raspberries and shouting ba-ba-ba at the top of their voice.

Your child goes through lots of stages to learn to talk. Babbling is a way to practise using their mouth, tongue, and lips to make words. By four to six months old, they will have developed the muscle strength in their mouth to close their lips together purposefully – and start changing the noises they produce. This allows them to start experimenting by making new sounds, often repetitive syllables like ba, pa, ma, and da.

Soon they will start mixing different sounds and creating sequences to try and copy the cadence of conversations, even if they can't form words yet. When they are between 10 and 14 months old, it is from these sounds that their first words will emerge.

WHAT YOU MIGHT BE THINKING

My baby is making so many funny sounds, sometimes so loudly! Are they just experimenting with making new noises or actually trying to say their first words? Should I mimic them – or only speak "proper" words to them.

WHAT THEY MIGHT BE THINKING

• **Your baby is watching you move your lips** to see how you make sounds. They may practise by smacking their lips together.

• **Since birth, your baby's vocal tract** has lengthened and they now have more control over their tongue. This means they can start to make a wider range of sounds and vocalizations.

• **Your baby may enjoy babbling** when they play alone. It's often a sign they are ready to play.

• **As your baby experiments** with making noises, they are listening to themselves carefully. They may try different volumes, perhaps by babbling into a toy bucket to hear their echo, as well as trying out raspberries and clicking sounds.

> ❝ ❞
> # AS YOUR BABY EXPERIMENTS WITH MAKING NOISES, THEY ARE LISTENING TO THEMSELVES CAREFULLY. THEY MAY TRY DIFFERENT VOLUMES, AS WELL AS RASPBERRY SOUNDS.

HOW YOU COULD RESPOND

In the moment

Repeat back the sounds
Show that what they are doing is important by repeating back the sounds your baby makes. Research has found that they will try harder to respond. "Strive for five" interactions as this will help them learn to talk and listen in conversations.

Look at them as you speak
Get face to face with them and exaggerate your lip movements as you say words. Wait a few seconds and pause for them to respond. Avoid rushing them so they don't feel pressured, and to show you are listening carefully.

Pay attention
Even if you can't understand the words your baby is saying, they have a clear idea of what they want to say. They will be trying to convey meaning and emotion, whether happy, sad, or excited.

In the long term

Respond in other ways
Babies may make as many as a thousand vocalizations every day. While you won't be able to respond every time, remember you can also acknowledge your baby's vocalizations with eye contact, smiling, or saying "aha", or "really?"

Offer interpretations
If you feel confident you can understand what your baby is trying to say from their eye contact, gestures, and the context, offer to name it for them. If they are babbling while looking at a ball, you could say: "That's a ball. Do you want it?"

Make animal words
Make animal sounds, like "Baa" for a sheep and "Moo" for a cow, with your baby as you play. This can be a fun way for them to communicate until they can form human words.

SEE RELATED TOPICS
Was that my baby's first word?: pp.112-113

"WHY DOES MY BABY LOVE TO BE HELD IN THE AIR?"

Even though babies come into the world relatively immobile, they enjoy the experience of movement as soon as they are born. Once they have stronger bodies, they may be ready to enjoy more adventurous games.

SCENARIO | Your baby is squealing with delight as you hold them above your head, as if they are flying like Superman.

When your baby was born they were curled up to fit snugly into your womb. Now they are out in the world, they have to learn how it feels to move their body in space. This is governed by their vestibular – or balance – system, which is based in their inner ears and sends signals to the parts of their brain that keep track of their body's position.

As they grow, different movements like being rocked, gently swung, and rolling will help them develop this sense. As their spine becomes less C-shaped and more S-shaped, they will also get a stronger core and can be held up. This offers them a whole new range of physical activities, like bouncing, swinging, and flying games.

WHAT YOU MIGHT BE THINKING

My baby is giggling so much, but is this flying game too soon and too adventurous for them?

SEE RELATED TOPICS
Why does my toddler love to take risks?: pp.146–147

WHAT THEY MIGHT BE THINKING

- **In the liquid bubble of the uterus,** your baby felt weightless. Now they are starting to understand how gravity works and will enjoy being held up.

- **Your baby is getting a stronger core,** but still has proportionally shorter legs, so it's easier for them to hold their body straight when you hold them up.

- **As they are zoomed around,** your baby is putting total trust in you. They may also be fearless because they do not yet know what it feels like to fall.

- **Your baby loves to connect with you** as you raise them up, because you are completely focussed on them, promoting laughter and bonding.

"Why does my baby love to be held in the air?"

HOW YOU COULD RESPOND

In the moment

Linger in these moments
Use this intense physical play to connect with your baby. Looking and smiling into your child's eyes creates high-intensity moments that will help bond you.

Keep it safe
When you move to more adventurous games, lift your baby but don't let go – or throw them. Never shake them or let their head roll back and forth.

Look out for overstimulation or distress
Watch for cues your baby is getting overwhelmed or have had too much, like tensing up, looking shocked, or grimacing.

In the long term

Start gently
At first experiment with different types of movement, depending on what your baby enjoys. For example, in the first months, you could try gently laying them on your inner forearm and rocking them back and forth. Or lie down with your knees tucked into your chest, then place your baby's tummy down on your shins and gently bounce them while holding their hands and singing to them.

Introduce swinging
From about eight months most babies can sit without support and will enjoy going on a baby swing at the park. Start by gently pushing from the front where they can see you, and say "hello" and "bye" as they swing.

Look into baby swimming
Swimming classes will boost a baby's sense of balance. Research has found that baby swimmers have better balance into early childhood.

> **THEY ARE STARTING TO UNDERSTAND HOW GRAVITY WORKS.**

"WHY DOES MY BABY LOVE BATH TIME SO MUCH?"

Bath time is not just about keeping your baby clean. It's also a way to offer a wide range of sensory experiences, boost their brain development, and have regular play and bonding time with your child.

SCENARIO | When you put your baby in the bath, they love playing with the bubbles and water so much they don't want to get out.

To start with, your baby may not love bath time. In their first three months, they are experiencing the world purely via their senses. The change of temperature and sensation, as well as the feeling of being suspended and exposed as they are lifted in and out of the water, can make them protest and cry. However, as their core strength and motor skills develop – so they can sit up and use both hands to splash and play with bath toys – it can become a playtime ritual you both look forward to. As part of a nightly routine, it can also become a sensory cue to let your baby know it will soon be bedtime.

> **WHAT YOU MIGHT BE THINKING**
>
> **Bath time seems to be** my baby's favourite time of day. Why do they adore it so much?

"Why does my baby love bath time so much?" 77

WHAT THEY MIGHT BE THINKING

- **Your baby often feels happy** in the bath because it's engaging all of their senses – from the touch, sight, and sound of the water to the smell of the soap and the taste of the water on their toys – helping them really focus on the experience.

- **As they get more confident** and used to bath times in their first year, your baby may grow to love this part of the day as a time when they can count on your undivided, screen-free attention.

- **By pouring water** from a container, your baby sees gravity in action, and by watching objects sink and float, they are learning about different materials.

> **" "**
> USE BUBBLES, BEAKERS, BATH CHALKS, AND WATERING CANS TO EXPAND THEIR GAMES.

HOW YOU COULD RESPOND

In the moment

Lower them carefully
To help a young baby stay calm until they get used to it, try to keep your body close to theirs as you bend over to lower them into the water. If this is not possible, cover them in a muslin cloth or flannel and use your hands to firmly support their head and bottom, in case they startle. Keep their heads above the level of their bodies while maintaining eye contact, and talking quietly so they can hear your voice.

Practise with another caregiver
Until you get comfortable with the logistics, ask your co-parent to be there to help – so your baby senses your confidence. Take turns being the main bath-giver so you can swap this role.

Prepare for after the bath
Have a hooded towel next to the bath, ready to wrap them in. You could also ease the transition by making your bathroom warmer and moving straight to a baby massage.

In the long term

Join them
To increase bonding and playtime, try getting in the tub with them. If they are not yet sitting, the support of your body and feel of your skin will help them feel more secure, particularly if you are moving them from a baby bath – in which they have felt more contained – to a big tub.

Use sense words
The routine of bath time lets you repeat lots of words and build on them. As your child gets older, talk out loud about what they are doing, whether it's pushing their boat or rubber duck. By describing each step of bath time too, like turning on the taps and getting undressed, you'll also teach them about sequencing – or learning how to do things in a logical order.

Add toys
As they grow, you can use bubbles, beakers, bath chalks, and watering cans to expand their games. To make it more enjoyable for you, give yourself something to kneel on as you play with your child in the bath. To make the clean-up easier, try using a plastic mesh basket to scoop out all the bath toys in one go.

SEE RELATED TOPICS
What does the world feel like to my baby?: pp.28-29

INTRODUCING SOLID FOODS

According to the World Health Organization, and many other health authorities, babies don't need to be given solid foods until around six months old.

From around four months, you may notice that your baby is getting increasingly interested in the foods you put in your mouth, and may stare or grab at them. This is not just because they love to copy you, but also because they are little explorers who love to use their tongues and lips to help them understand the world. By this point, they are likely to have doubled their birth weight. As a result, they need more calories, so they are feeling hungrier, too.

It's time to look for the signs that your child is ready to move to more solid foods.

1
Check if they are ready
Can your child sit in a feeding chair without toppling over? Do they swallow more food than they spit out? They don't need teeth because they can use their gums to break up food.

4
Offer variety
It can take between five and 15 tries of the same food before babies may start to like it. Furthermore, babies are first reared on sweet milks. Give them time to adjust to a wider range of flavours.

> **FOOD IS THE ULTIMATE TOY. YOUR CHILD CAN LICK, SQUEEZE, MUSH, AND SMEAR IT.**

WORKING THINGS OUT

8 key principles

2
See food from their point of view
Look for cues that they are enjoying it or have had enough. Take them out of their chair when they are showing signs of boredom, so they associate mealtimes with fun.

3
See it as exploration
Human babies are wired to be cautious when they first eat solids, in case they are poisonous. It makes sense for them to use their senses of smell, sight, and touch before deciding to put anything new in their mouths.

5
Make it comfortable
Look for a feeding chair with a footrest or that's on the floor so their feet are not dangling. Otherwise, their torso and tummy will be distended, making it harder to eat and swallow. Consider putting a washable mat or newspaper underneath so it's easier to clean up after.

6
Take an easy-going approach
If your child is absorbed in trying a new food, don't interrupt. Avoid rushing it. Let them work out for themselves how they feel and how much they want. As your baby is still mainly being nourished with milk, see any extra solid foods they eat as an "add on". Never insist they eat everything on their tray or plate.

7
Let them be messy
To your child, food is the ultimate toy. They can lick, squeeze, mush, and smear it. Wait until the end of the feeding session before wiping their face. This phase is not about teaching your baby manners. It's about getting them to enjoy and trust food.

8
Eat with them
Your baby loves to copy you and will be observing you biting, chewing, and swallowing. They will also feel included and learn that family meals are a time to enjoy food and be sociable together.

TAILORED ADVICE

Offer cutlery
To start with, your baby's main tools for eating should be their hands. You can also offer them a spoon to suck on and play with. Load one up and see if they want to put it in their mouth.

Make it brief
Keep the first sessions short, offering just one or two foods they can explore and grasp with their hands, like strips (cut to the size of your little finger) of pear, avocado, or soft, cooked carrot.

Don't play games
Avoid "playing aeroplanes" and trying to sneak food into their open mouths when they are not looking. It's better for your child to take charge of the process for themselves.

Don't confuse gagging with choking
When your baby tries new solid foods, they may gag because they are learning how much they chew and swallow, and how different textures and tastes feel. This is a protective mechanism, which will make them retch and cough and go red.

"WHY IS MY BABY CRAWLING LIKE THAT?"

By seven to 12 months, your baby's growing strength and coordination mean they are ready to crawl, but they may choose different ways to do this. They don't care how they get going. They just want to move.

SCENARIO | Instead of doing the "classic crawl" of alternating both hands and knees to move forward, your baby is shuffling on their bottom.

Crawling is their first big adventure, because now they can start to explore anything that interests them. This milestone depends on a lot of different skills coming together – including strength, balance, and stability, as well as the motor development that allows them to coordinate their limbs. However, infants don't all crawl the same way.

They may use a mixture of techniques based on what's easiest and quickest in the moment. This may depend on your flooring, as some surfaces give better traction than others. Clothing also plays a part, as some outfits will allow them to move more freely. However your child crawls, they are now on track for more complex movements, like pulling up to stand.

WHAT YOU MIGHT BE THINKING

What a funny way to crawl. Is that OK? Should they be crawling the "normal" way?

SEE RELATED TOPICS
Why does my baby move their body like that?: pp.30-31

WHAT THEY MIGHT BE THINKING

• **For months your baby had to view the world** from the floor. A new vantage point drives them to move forward and explore.

• **To start with, your infant may pull themselves forward** using their arms, commando style. If they don't like the feeling of being on their tummy, they may bounce along on their bottom.

• **Before they start crawling**, they may stay still on all fours, rocking back and forth, before finally setting off, perhaps to get a toy that's just out of reach.

• **Now they are mobile**, they are getting to grips with obstacles, and using hand–eye coordination. As crawling uses lots of energy, they may also be hungrier.

"Why is my baby crawling like that?" 81

HOW YOU COULD RESPOND

In the moment

Get down on the floor
Crawling will open up many more ways to play with your baby. Meeting them face to face on the floor will delight them. You can play chase the ball, or offer them a large cardboard box, open at both ends, to crawl through.

Consider their clothing
Your baby may have developed their crawl in response to their clothing. For example, dresses can get caught under their knees, bringing them to a halt. At times, their nappy may get in the way. Consider letting them try crawling nappy-free to free up their movement.

Embrace their style
Babies will try different styles of crawling. By the time they walk, you won't be able to tell which ways they used.

Think about your flooring
Your baby may find it easier to slither if they are mainly playing on smooth surfaces like floorboards. A carpet or rug may offer them more traction. As they get going, offer different surfaces, like grass and sand.

Let their feet touch the floor
Shoes and socks can prevent your baby from feeling the surface and getting a grip. When they are not barefoot, put them in non-slip socks or thin-soled flexible shoes.

In the long term

Let them find out what's safe
Babies need to learn what is risky and what is not by trial and error. Be on hand to help them negotiate steps, slopes, gaps, and different surfaces as they learn. But don't intervene too much unless you have to. Eye tracking research has found that your baby will also stop to look at the expression on your face to help work out what's safe.

Don't worry if they skip this stage
About one in 15 babies skips crawling and goes straight to pulling themselves up on furniture and "cruising" along it. As long as they have reached other milestones like sitting up, accept it as their style.

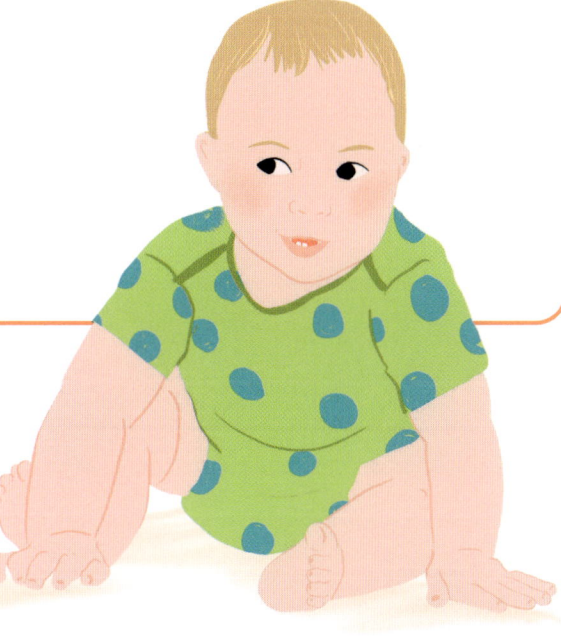

"WHAT WORDS CAN MY BABY UNDERSTAND?"

Even though they haven't spoken their first word yet, your baby has now heard enough language to isolate and understand some of the words and phrases they hear the most.

SCENARIO | When you say "bye", your baby waves. They also look at you when you say "No!" if they reach out to grab a glass that could break.

Your baby is starting to pick out words and basic phrases from the jumble they hear every hour. They have also worked out that words represent things they are interested in. The first words they are likely to understand will be the most important things in their lives, as well as basic commands they hear often. These are likely to include their own name, because you look at them when you say it to get their attention, "no", and words for favourite foods, such as "milk".

They can understand more than they can say, but it will take more motor skill development in their lips and mouth – as well as lots of practice babbling – before they are ready to form words.

WHAT YOU MIGHT BE THINKING

Wow, they really seem to understand a lot of what I am saying. Do I have to start watching what I say?

WHAT THEY MIGHT BE THINKING

• **While your baby** may not be able to say the words yet, they will increasingly show their understanding with gestures, like waving when you say "bye".

• **Your baby wants to please you**, so if you give them simple instructions like "Give it to Daddy", they may hand over the object to him. If you say "No!" when they are exploring something you don't want them to touch, they may now pause and look at you to see why.

• **When your child learns to point** with their index finger, they will start to direct your attention to the new things they want you to name for them.

• **Your baby may categorize a broad range of objects** under the same word. For example, they may think "cat" describes any four-legged animal.

HOW YOU COULD RESPOND

In the moment

Follow their interests
Pay attention to what they are looking and pointing at. They will learn best if you follow their gaze, rather than name things that have not yet caught their eye.

Hold objects at your eye level
If you want to help your baby learn the word for an object, look directly at your child, and hold the object, like an apple, at eye level, so they can see it next to your lips forming the word; this is now a key part of their language learning.

Isolate words
Help your baby identify words by playing peek-a-boo. For example, you could hide a dinosaur under a scarf, pull it away, and say, "Dinosaur" several times. Keep it playful and move on when your baby gets bored.

Keep it simple
If you are naming an object for your baby, isolate the noun and repeat it without adding adjectives or verbs. For now, nouns will be the anchors for learning the rest of speech.

In the long term

Read lots of books
Pointing at pictures and naming what you see will expose your baby to new words. Help them learn meanings by doing actions for songs like "Row The Boat" and "Incy Wincy Spider".

Connect while talking to them
Your baby needs to see the direction your eyes are looking, as well as your expressions, to help them understand what you are saying. Avoid looking down at your phone when you are with them so they know you are interested in what they are doing.

Teach simple signs
Your child already has the motor skills to make simple gestures. Giving them simple baby signs will help them feel understood. These could include putting your hands to your mouth to mean "Eat" or bunching your fingers and tapping them together to say "More". If you demonstrate this enough, they are likely to learn to do the same.

SEE RELATED TOPICS
Why does my toddler say no all the time?: pp.134-135

"WHAT DOES MY BABY SEE IN THE MIRROR?"

When your baby first looks in the mirror, they won't recognize themselves. It will take several stages of development before they realize that the image they see is a reflection of their unique appearance.

SCENARIO | When your child looks in a full-length mirror, they smile and point at their reflection.

When your baby is born, they have no concept of themselves as a separate person from you. And, of course, they have no idea how light and reflection work. Your baby will think they are seeing another infant when they look in the mirror. In their second year, your toddler will slowly work out that the reflection in the mirror has too much in common with them – from wearing the same clothes to making the same movements – for it not to be an image of them. However, it's not until they nearly turn two that most children are able to point to themselves when they are asked: "Who's that in the mirror?"

WHAT YOU MIGHT BE THINKING

Do they know that's them? Or do they think it's another baby?

SEE RELATED TOPICS
Does my baby recognize me?: pp.50-51,
What is my baby staring at?: pp.58-59

WHAT THEY MIGHT BE THINKING

- **When they first see their reflection**, your new baby will recognize the image as another baby – and may gaze, smile, and make cooing sounds at it, thinking it's a friendly playmate.

- **From around six to 18 months**, your baby may try to kiss and hug the reflection – or go behind the mirror to find the other child.

- **If they see you in the mirror too**, they may wave at your reflection, but won't appear to be upset or confused by the other version of you on the glass.

- **By about 18 months your toddler** will link themselves with their reflection. They may wave or touch their nose to see if the child in the mirror does the same.

"What does my baby see in the mirror?"

> **YOUR BABY MAY TRY TO KISS AND HUG THE REFLECTION.**

HOW YOU COULD RESPOND

In the moment

Offer a baby-safe mirror
Young babies love watching faces. Looking at their reflection will keep them entertained.

Help them develop depth perception
Try moving a small mirror closer to their faces and then further away, so they practise shifting focus.

Be in the mirror with them
Your child will start to understand that mirrors reflect people if you look in one together. They see your face more often than theirs and will recognize you quickly.

Help them develop self-awareness
Try showing your baby their reflection in the mirror and ask: "Who's that?" Then say their name, point to the reflection and say: "Yes, it's you!" and then their name again. Research shows the more they see their faces, the sooner they will recognize themselves.

In the long term

Teach toddlers to name body parts
Encourage your baby to touch the body parts as you name them. Research has found that babies and toddlers who were shown how to touch their faces when looking in the mirror will recognize their reflections two months earlier, probably because it helps them understand that they are a separate person.

Try the mirror test
As part of a game in the middle of their second year, try playfully putting a small dollop of paint or blusher on your toddler's nose to see if they try to touch or rub the mark off when they see their reflection. If they rub at the mark on their own nose, it means they now recognize the reflection in the mirror is them.

"WHY DOES MY BABY LIKE NURSERY RHYMES?"

To your baby, the nursery rhymes and lullabies you sing to them are more than just songs. They are ways to learn language and bond with you.

SCENARIO | When your baby is in their highchair, you notice they turn their head to look at you when they hear you sing "Twinkle, Twinkle, Little Star".

As soon as your baby was born, you probably noticed them pay attention when you talked to them in a high-pitched, sing-song tone. As you realized how much you could engage them emotionally this way, it was a natural next step to sing them nursery rhymes when they were playful, or lullabies to help them fall asleep. It's not just the tune of the nursery rhyme your baby is responding to. Studies have shown that parents tend to be more emotionally engaged with and bonded to their babies when they sing to them. Your child will pick up on this, making them love these songs more.

WHAT YOU MIGHT BE THINKING

I can't hold a tune at all, and I sound awful. Does my baby really like me singing like this? Do I sound silly?

WHAT THEY MIGHT BE THINKING

- **Babies love nursery rhymes** because their predictable structure helps them spot patterns and know what comes next. This helps them decode language and start to understand their world.

- **If you sang a particular nursery rhyme** while you were pregnant, your child is likely to prefer it now.

Studies have found that babies can recognize tunes they heard in utero up to a year later.

- **Your baby will love a song** sung in a happy, upbeat way in a high-pitched voice the most, according to research. Around four or five months old, you may notice your infant is babbling in the same pitch.

SEE RELATED TOPICS
Why does my toddler love to sing and dance?: pp.184–185

HOW YOU COULD RESPOND

In the moment

Keep it simple
Babies can't yet screen out background noise, so sing them simple songs in a quiet room to help them listen.

Sing it solo
Research has found babies prefer the solo human voice. Don't rely on recordings – your baby wants to hear you.

Introduce actions
Babies and toddlers are more likely to remember words to songs if they learn actions, too. At first, gently move their limbs along to songs like "Pat-a-cake" and "Wind the Bobbin Up", until they can do it themselves.

Repeat their favourites
In the early months, your baby will prefer a repetitive song, so they can predict what's coming next.

In the long term

Make lullabies part of their sleep ritual
Studies have found babies exposed to happy music sleep and smile more. Lullabies at bedtime have also been found to lower the heart rates of both parent and child and encourage better sleep. At stressful moments, like immunizations, they have also been found to lower a baby's pain.

Use songs to change the mood
Singing to your baby can change their mood quickly, particularly when you need to calm them down or they are resistant to getting dressed or having their nappy changed. Keep special songs for certain times of the day, like waking up, brushing their teeth, or bath time, to help children know what's coming next and to ease transitions.

" KEEP SPECIAL SONGS FOR CERTAIN TIMES, LIKE WAKING UP.

PARENTS' SURVIVAL GUIDE

TWINS

Twins and multiple babies are almost always together because they share the same space from conception. As infants, they give each other comfort, warmth, and companionship.

Because they communicate naturally, twins and triplets may also talk later, studies have found. At times, it may feel to you like they are more attached to each other than to you. But remember your babies each need their individual bond with you as their adult caregiver to develop their separate identities. With a bit of planning, and extra help, there will be ways for them to form their own unique relationship with you.

1
Encourage individuality
Think of your babies not so much as "The Twins", but as babies born at the same time. Set out to treat them as different children with their own personalities from the outset.

4
Let them co-sleep
When they are put down together, research has found that multiples touch, hug, and suck on each other. This has the same effect as being held by you. They tend to develop similar sleep patterns, and wake less in their first three months.

> " TREAT THEM AS DIFFERENT CHILDREN WITH THEIR OWN PERSONALITIES. "

WORKING THINGS OUT

8 key principles

2
Make them visually different
If it's not obvious which twin is which, keep their hospital identity tags on until it becomes easier to tell them apart – and from then on dress them in different coloured clothes. Take pictures of them separately so you, and others, don't see them as "a unit."

3
Help them build their identities
As they grow, pause, and use their different names at the start of each sentence when you look at them, to underline they are different people.

5
Teach turn-taking early
Your babies will need to wait their turn. Let them know this will happen reliably and predictably. Let the other one watch, while you talk. For example, you could say, "Mia, FIRST I will change your nappy. Noah, NEXT I will change yours," emphasizing the before and after words.

6
Give daily one-on-one time
Set out with your co-parent, if you have one, to make a routine so you each get daily one-on-one playtime with your babies, even if it's just 15 minutes a day. This will also help each infant learn that they can predictably enjoy activities separately from their twin and be sure of their relationship with you.

7
Talk about how to share the care
Research shows that raising twins is much easier when both parents are equally involved. One parent will find it very hard to meet the needs of two or more babies consistently. Don't be afraid to invite trusted and willing family and friends to help.

8
Swap caring roles
Twins may attach themselves more to one parent than the other to get individual time. This may cause problems later if one twin only wants to be cared for by one parent. Try to swap caring roles so they have undivided attention from, and are securely attached to, both parents.

TAILORED ADVICE

Free up time
To form a strong attachment, your babies need one-on-one time with you. For the first year or two, don't feel guilty about putting other things – like a tidy home – on hold until your babies become more independent.

Give special thought to older siblings
Twins will have much more of an impact on an older child than a single sibling, so make sure they still feel special. Avoid sending the message that they "should" be extra excited because two babies are coming instead of one. To a young child, this will sound like double the number of rivals to take you away. Even though you need an extra pair of hands, don't turn them into gophers, which could make them feel sidelined.

"WHY DOES MY BABY FIND THAT FUNNY?"

Laughing with your baby isn't just a way to have fun. It's one of the ways they communicate with you before they can talk. Observing what they find humorous is also a useful window into their developing understanding of the world.

SCENARIO | Your baby starts to laugh hysterically when you start sneezing.

Your baby's giggles at about three or four months will be reinforced when you laugh back. At first your baby may laugh because they enjoy a physical sensation, like being bounced on your knee. As they learn how the world works, they will start to be amused when things happen outside the norm.

By about six months old, 60 per cent of babies laugh at the absurd antics of their parents – pulling faces or making silly noises. By about 11 months, half of babies make up their own jokes, such as lifting their top to show you their belly button, doing a funny dance, or blowing raspberries.

WHAT YOU MIGHT BE THINKING

What's happening in their little brain that now makes them think everything I do is so funny?

SEE RELATED TOPICS
Why does my baby love peakaboo?: pp.92-93

WHAT THEY MIGHT BE THINKING

◉ **Your baby will quickly learn laughing** is a way to keep you playing with them. They realize you are sharing an experience, and they have your full attention.

◉ **Laughing makes them feel good**, due to the release of endorphins and the bonding hormone oxytocin, released when you share an experience.

◉ **They will laugh most** with trusted caregivers, followed by siblings and often animals. If a stranger plays the same game with them, it could trigger tears because it doesn't feel as safe.

◉ **Deviations from the norm** will make your baby laugh. They may laugh at things that surprise them, like you sneezing or hiccupping.

"Why does my baby find that funny?"

> **LAUGHTER ACTIVATES REWARD PATHWAYS IN THE BRAIN AND REDUCES STRESS.**

HOW YOU COULD RESPOND

In the moment

Start humour gently
With young babies you could start with a playful game that involves gentle touch, like "Round and Round the Garden". Blow raspberries on their cheeks or try a quiet game of peekaboo.

Introduce more surprises
When your baby gets an idea of how you are "supposed" to behave, from about six months onwards, they will laugh when things go differently. Make them laugh by doing unexpected things, like pretending their toy dinosaur can talk or the cat is saying "woof".

Follow their lead
Your baby will need to be in the right mood for playing and laughing. Look for cues they are getting frightened or overwhelmed. A crumpled expression on baby's face will tell you they've had enough.

In the long term

Mirror your child's humour
In these first years, your baby's humour is developing fast. Notice what they find funny so you can reflect it back and enter into their world. If your humour is too sophisticated, they could get confused.

Make humour part of family life
Laughter activates reward pathways in the brain, boosts immunity, and reduces stress – for everyone in the family. It's also an important social skill for your child to have in their future relationships.

Use laughter to change the mood
As your child starts to test boundaries as a toddler, you can use laughter to change the tone. If they don't want to get in the pram, for example, you could suggest that it's actually a train, and it's their turn to drive it. Set off with lots of "choo choo" noises. If they don't want to change their nappy, make them laugh by using a clean one as a hat.

"WHY DOES MY BABY LOVE PEEKABOO?"

Peekaboo is a universal game for babies. As well as being fun, it's a powerful learning tool to help them develop everything from memory to motor skills.

SCENARIO | Your baby laughs every time you hide your face behind a blanket, and you pull it off to reveal your face again.

From four to seven months, your child's memory is improving. They are starting to work out that even if you, or an object, are not visible, you're still somewhere in the world.

Peekaboo is a game that can evolve with your child. When you first play it, your baby will look surprised when you reappear. As they get more control over their movements, they can initiate the game by pulling a blanket up and down to hide their face from you. This shows they are learning to imagine the world from your point of view – and they will be delighted they can make you laugh.

WHAT YOU MIGHT BE THINKING

Why do they find this game so hysterically funny? It seems pretty repetitive to me!

SEE RELATED TOPICS
Why does my baby find that funny?: pp.90-91

WHAT THEY MIGHT BE THINKING

- **Because they love you,** each time your baby sees you again, it makes them happy. The game needs your undivided attention, it also helps your child feel connected to you.

- **As your baby waits for you to respond** and vice versa, this helps them learn how conversation works. The to-and-fro makes them feel like equal partners.

- **Peekaboo is only funny** for your child when they can anticipate what happens next. Every time you pop back into view, you confirm their prediction that you are coming back.

- **Flap books offer a similar surprise.** As your baby develops "object permanence", they will also love "posting" things, and opening and closing doors.

HOW YOU COULD RESPOND

In the moment

Give the game subtitles
Help your baby develop language skills by adding words as you play, like "Hello", "Bye", and "Where did I go?" and "Here I am!" as you appear and disappear.

Take turns
As you take turns to hide your face, your baby is also practising turn-taking, a key skill in conversation that is important when they start to make friends at school. Use a light scarf as a screen so your baby can easily remove it from your face or their own. This will help develop their muscular coordination and learn more about cause and effect.

Play hide-and-seek
As your child gets more mobile, you can also play hide-and-seek with them by hiding yourself or their toys around the room and encouraging them to search.

In the long term

Use it to ease separation anxiety
Peekaboo can also teach your child that if you go away, you will always come back. This can help prepare them for separations, like going to nursery.

Build the tension
The build-up before you reveal yourself increases dopamine levels in your baby's brain. Vary how long you take between "peeka" and "boo", encouraging your baby to fill in the gap.

> "" ""
> YOUR BABY IS ALSO PRACTISING TURN-TAKING, A KEY SKILL IN CONVERSATION.

"WHY DOES MY BABY DROP FOOD?"

If you are giving your baby solid foods to try, you may find that they are just as interested in throwing and dropping it from their highchair, as eating it.

SCENARIO | Most of the food you've prepared for your baby has ended up on the floor, leaving you with a big clear-up job.

Now your baby is trying solid foods and has the hand-eye coordination to feed themselves, food may become their new toy. There are several reasons. After developing the pincer grip to pick small things up between thumb and forefingers, at around eight and 10 months, they learn how to let things go voluntarily. When they realize that moving their arms as they drop makes it go even further, they will find it fun to lob it out of their highchair. Your baby will also be fascinated by dropping food to see what happens when different weights and textures hit the ground.

WHAT YOU MIGHT BE THINKING

What a mess! Shouldn't my baby be eating food, not throwing it?

SEE RELATED TOPICS
Why won't my toddler eat their dinner?: pp.130–131

WHAT THEY MIGHT BE THINKING

- **Now they are trying solids**, your baby is programmed to use their senses to investigate the foods you give them. This means tasting, smelling, and watching it fall.

- **Your baby loves seeing cause and effect**. They may be interested to lean over the edge of their highchair to see where it's gone and how it looks.

- **They may throw food off** because they are no longer hungry or there's too much food in front of them.

- **If you're doing something else** while your baby is in their highchair, throwing food gets your attention. Seeing you run over or pull a face is fun if they are bored of being in their highchair.

HOW YOU COULD RESPOND

In the moment

Get perspective
Your baby is not making a mess to make your job harder. Let it go. It's a phase that will pass.

Keep it positive
If you think throwing food is a sign your child has had enough, you could say, "You dropped your raspberries. They've gone splat! Raspberries are for eating though. When you throw, it tells me it's time to put them away."

Check if your baby has eaten enough
Your baby may be throwing food because they are bored. Look out for other cues, like turning their head away, banging on their tray, and squealing more than they eat.

Head off mess
Reduce the mess to clean up afterwards. Put a mat under your child's highchair, or newspaper you can throw away. Pick up food only after your baby has finished eating.

In the long term

Tweak mealtimes
There are ways to limit the mess. Offer smaller portions. Serve their food directly on their tray, so bowls don't go overboard. A highchair makes food-dropping more entertaining, so try a lower feeding chair or toddler seat.

Take it outside
If your baby is at a particularly messy stage and there's the weather for it, take them outside for a picnic.

Experiment too
If your child is more interested in playing with food than eating it, sit with them on the floor and play along. Sniff it, squish it, and mould it into new shapes. Pick a time when they are not hungry, so they play rather than eat.

Redirect their throwing
Let them throw other things, like a bouncy ball. Your child will be fascinated by how objects fly and where they land.

❝ ❞

SIT WITH THEM ON THE FLOOR AND PLAY ALONG.

PARENTS' SURVIVAL GUIDE

PLAY

Play is not only one of the most natural things your child will do – it's also one of the most important. Play is how they learn everything including how to move their bodies and relate to other people.

It boosts your baby's brain development in every conceivable way, helping them to develop concentration, imagination, and problem-solving skills, as well as lowering their levels of stress. Best of all, as a parent, all you need to do is allow them space and time for your child to do as much as possible. Play starts the moment your baby returns your eye contact, smiles at you, or babbles back at you. View it as something that's a natural part of your everyday life with your child, not a separate add-on. Over the coming years, it will be one of the best ways to connect with your child and help them feel good about themselves.

1
Let your child lead
Allow them to get into the flow without asking too many questions. Observe, smile, and occasionally comment, so they feel noticed. Join in or copy them when they ask you.

4
Create "yes" spaces
Look for a way to create an enclosed play space, where you don't have to constantly say no. You could put a box at your child's level, filled with household objects like utensils, soft brushes, shells, and a baby-safe mirror, to see what they are drawn to.

> **OVER THE COMING YEARS, IT WILL BE ONE OF THE BEST WAYS TO CONNECT WITH YOUR CHILD.**

WORKING THINGS OUT
8 key principles

2
Avoid trying to "teach" them
Babies learn best when they are enjoying themselves. Your child can only master their next skill when they have mastered their last – and even young babies can sense when you are following your agenda, not theirs.

3
Weave play into everyday life
Avoid seeing play as something you "do" with your child. Young children naturally love to help and copy you. So, whether it's asking for their help to wash vegetables or sort the laundry, get your child involved and make it playful.

5
Encourage physical play
Young mammals play-fight to develop strength and survival skills. In the same way, rough-and-tumble play with a caregiver offers valuable ways for young children to feel powerful, learn their limits, regulate their emotions, and get rid of any aggression they can't express with words.

6
Allow repetition
Playing with young children may feel dull because it is repetitive. But doing things over and over is essential for your child to gain mastery of new skills, whether it's rolling a ball or a simple puzzle. The more closely you observe your child manipulating and exploring different toys and objects, the more interesting their play is.

7
Keep toys simple
The more a toy does, the less your child has to do. Simple toys – like different-sized balls or blocks – let your child decide how to play. Adapt household materials too. Cardboard boxes can be used by your child to make anything from a car to a house.

8
Circulate toys
Young children can get stressed and find it hard to focus if they feel surrounded by too many toys. When they have fewer, research has found they play with them in more varied ways and for longer. When you rotate toys, check with your child so a favourite doesn't suddenly disappear.

TAILORED ADVICE

Play movement games
From blowing raspberries on their tummies to playing pat-a-cake, and dancing with them, physical games can help your child build muscle strength and coordination.

Make their play real-world
Your child learns best now from interacting in the real world, not screens. Educational games and apps – designed with lots of colours, movement, and noise – can reward children too quickly and encourage them to prefer screens over real world play.

Let them create their own worlds
Small children spend their lives directed by grown-ups. Give them opportunities to create their own small worlds where they direct what happens, whether it's moving figures around in a sand tray or creating a farm with toy animals on the carpet.

"WHY IS MY BABY NOW AFRAID OF STRANGERS?"

While your baby was happy to be held by other people for their first six months, they are now becoming wary and starting to cry when they see people they don't know as well.

SCENARIO | Your baby used to coo and smile when they saw their grandparents – but after several weeks apart, they cry when they come to visit.

Your child has grown up relying on you as their main caregiver. As they become more aware of the world around them, they are now noticing there are other people who they don't know as well – and that they feel safest with you.

As they develop a clear preference, they will start to feel wary of people they don't know as well, from about six to eight months old. While it may be embarrassing, see it as a normal part of their development. Stranger anxiety tends to peak between 12 to 15 months, and usually fades gradually as toddlers learn they can cope if they spend time without you.

WHAT YOU MIGHT BE THINKING

I am worried I can't leave my child with anyone. A few weeks ago, my baby was happy to go to anybody. Now they burst into tears and it's embarrassing.

WHAT THEY MIGHT BE THINKING

- **Your baby now has clearer eyesight** and a better memory. They can recognize people they know well from those they don't.

- **Fear of strangers** is wired into your baby for evolutionary reasons, so when they become more mobile, and start crawling or walking, they do not wander too far from their main protectors.

- **Your baby now recognizes** how dependent they are on you – and that not everyone will look after them in the special way you do.

- **If they realize** they are being left with a new caregiver they may cry loudly, get very fussy, go quiet, or look scared. They may turn away and nuzzle into you to feel safe again.

HOW YOU COULD RESPOND

In the moment

Show your child they are safe
Your baby is watching your eyes and expression for how to respond. Use your smile to give them reassurance that these new people are safe and friendly. Staying calm will also help your baby stay relaxed and happy.

Offer the safety of your arms
Introduce new people when you're holding your child. Be their secure base, which will allow them time to get used to the sight of new people. Give them time to observe and reach out to newcomers in their own time.

Explain it's not personal
Family members won't immediately know what stage of development your child is at. Let them know your child is now more wary of others and it's not personal, but a normal part of their developing attachment.

In the long term

Show your own social skills
Your child is watching to see how you interact with other people. Let them see you smile and chat to other people when you are out and about, so they also feel more confident meeting new people.

Share the care
For most of human history, babies have been cared for by several generations of the same family. Give your baby lots of experience with other family members so they can start forming strong attachments beyond you. Research shows relationships with grandparents have a long-term positive impact on children's happiness.

SEE RELATED TOPICS
When will my baby stop crying?: pp.52-53,
Separation anxiety: pp.124-125

> " "
> **IF THEY ARE BEING LEFT WITH A NEW CAREGIVER THEY MAY TURN AWAY AND NUZZLE INTO YOU TO FEEL SAFE AGAIN.**

"WHY DOES MY BABY POINT AT EVERYTHING?"

Now that they can control their hands, and isolate the use of their fingers, your baby will start pointing at things. This gesture is a milestone because it's an exciting new way for them to communicate with you.

SCENARIO | When you are at the park, your baby keeps pointing at the sky and babbling as if they want to show you something.

By around nine months old, your baby can move their fingers separately and make a pointing gesture, so they can show you specific things that interest them, known as "joint attention".

Babies will point for one of two reasons. They are either trying to say, "That looks interesting. What is it?" (known as declarative pointing), or they will point at things to tell you, "I like that. Can you bring it to me?", (known as imperative pointing). Pointing is a milestone because it gives your baby some control, and they are starting to understand other people's points of view. It will trigger an explosion in their language understanding if you name what they are showing you.

WHAT YOU MIGHT BE THINKING

My baby keeps pointing at things, but I'm not sure what. Is it a bird or a plane or a cloud? I'm delighted they are interested in the things around them, but I can't look up every time.

WHAT THEY MIGHT BE THINKING

• **Your baby is developing "theory of mind"**. They have worked out that they are separate individuals from you, and they can notice things that you can't. Now they realize this, they want you to see what they see too.

• **Your baby feels good when** you turn to look where they are pointing. This shows them they can make things happen and their view of the world is important.

• **After your baby has pointed** and looked at the thing they are interested in, they are likely to look back at your face to check you are looking at it too.

• **Because you name the things they are interested in**, your baby is suddenly learning lots of new words. Studies show that babies who point more go on to have a wide vocabulary and use longer sentences.

SEE RELATED TOPICS
What is my baby staring at?: pp.58-59

HOW YOU COULD RESPOND

In the moment

Take lots of interest
Look at what your baby is pointing at and name it. You can also raise your eyebrows, gasp, and smile, which will make them feel good.

Be patient
You may feel exhausted by your child's constant requests to look at what they are pointing at. Bear in mind your baby is on a quest for information and the world is an exciting place.

Point things out to them
Lift them out of their pram on walks and point out specific things, like a plane in the sky or an interesting bird. You can name things in new detail, such as the tail of a cat or the wheel of a bus.

In the long term

Enourage other hand activities
Being able to use their fingers separately is a key skill in holding pencils and learning to write and draw. You could show them finger painting, which builds fine motor skills in their hands.

Play pointing games
Make it fun by helping them to use their index finger to point at and pop bubbles. This will also boost hand–eye coordination.

Use pointing to boost memory
Your baby will now remember things they saw on previous walks. You could point to the place you saw a squirrel yesterday to see if they remember.

> **" "**
> BECAUSE YOU NAME THINGS, YOUR BABY IS SUDDENLY LEARNING LOTS OF NEW WORDS.

"WHY DOES MY BABY LOVE TO BANG AND CLAP?"

As a little scientist, your baby loves to see how what they do affects the world around them. With more control of their arms and hands, they are delighted to discover that when they hit a surface, it makes a noise.

SCENARIO | Instead of using their spoon to eat at mealtimes, your baby loves to bang it on their highchair tray.

Now that your baby can sit up, they are excited to use the newfound dexterity in their arms and hands to make things happen. They realize that using an object, such as a spoon, to strike a surface makes an even louder sound than their hands.

Your baby may also bring their hands together to clap. If they see you clap to music, they will try to do the same. Though your baby's banging and clapping may sound random, they have an inbuilt sense of rhythm. Even newborns can pick out the beat of a nursery rhyme. As they grow older, developing this ability – by giving your child things to bang and songs to clap along to – will help them spot patterns in language and learn to talk.

WHAT YOU MIGHT BE THINKING

What a racket! I was hoping they'd use that spoon to put food in their mouth. I can't take them out to eat any more because they bang on the table so much.

SEE RELATED TOPICS
What can my baby hear?: pp.38–39

WHAT THEY MIGHT BE THINKING

◉ **Banging helps your baby** understand that hard things – like saucepans – make more noise than soft. Exploring volume and tempo will help them grasp that talking can be fast and slow, too.

◉ **The louder the noise they make**, the more you take notice – and your child may do it to get your attention at mealtimes.

◉ **Your baby may struggle** at first to bring their hands together accurately enough to clap. They will keep trying to copy you.

◉ **When you bang or clap to a song** with your child, it triggers reward chemicals. Research has found that drumming with children makes them less defiant and improves communication.

HOW YOU COULD RESPOND

In the moment

Encourage them
Give your baby opportunities to drum at other times, by giving range of objects to hit, like a set of saucepans. Offer lots of smiles and praise.

Play along
Your baby is keen to copy you. See if they can copy the number of beats and claps you make.

Take turns banging and clapping
Having a musical conversation with your baby will help build their conversation skills when they start to talk. It will also sharpen their attention and listening abilities.

In the long term

Offer a range of instruments
If the noise of banging on a highchair tray or a saucepan is too much, offer softer instruments such as plastic containers, or try a xylophone.

Vary the tempo
As your child starts learning to talk, you can also bang out a rhythm of difficult, longer words to help break them down into syllables.

Show them loud and softs
If you are out and about and need to be quieter to fit into a social environment, distract your baby with quieter clapping games or softer singing games. This will help them learn they can make noise at different levels.

❝ ❞

IF THE NOISE IS TOO MUCH, OFFER SOFTER INSTRUMENTS SUCH AS PLASTIC CONTAINERS.

"WHY DOES MY BABY HATE NAPPY CHANGING?"

Nappy changing is an everyday task which can be a messy chore, even when your baby is staying put. It may feel like more of a challenge once your child is more mobile.

SCENARIO | Now your baby is crawling, they roll over to get away when you try to change their nappy, turning it into a frustrating battle of wills.

By six months old your baby probably only needs four to five nappy changes a day. As they become stronger and more mobile, they may not want to stay still when you change them.

As they become more independent, your baby may also start seeing nappy changes as an interruption to the fun they are having playing. Resisting may also be a way for your child to assert their independence and test boundaries. By looking at nappy changing as a regular chance to bond, and giving them some control over the process, you can help turn nappy changing from a battle of wills into a moment of connection.

> ### WHAT YOU MIGHT BE THINKING
>
> **When my baby has a dirty nappy,** I have to change it. Should I force them? It's making me worried about going out in case they need a change.

WHAT THEY MIGHT BE THINKING

● **Now your baby has so much more control** over their body, being picked up when they are playing and having to stay still can feel annoying. They may also dislike the sensation of having some of their clothes removed and lying down on a cold surface.

● **A nappy may feel bulky and constrictive** around the legs and hips to a mobile baby. They may prefer the freedom of not wearing one at all, and so resist when you put a new one on.

● **As modern nappies are more absorbent**, your child may not feel wet or uncomfortable enough for the bother of getting a new one. They want to decide, not you.

● **Your child tunes into your feelings.** If you talk about changing their nappy as inconvenient, dirty, or smelly, your child may start to feel the same way.

HOW YOU COULD RESPOND

In the moment

Reframe it
See nappy changing as a chance to give your child your undivided attention. You could play games that make it fun for them to keep still, like sleeping lions. While it won't always be possible, aim to have one or two nappy changes a day with some playtime. Finish with a kiss and a thank you.

Be gentle but firm
If you have limited time, you could say, "I see you don't want to change your nappy. It has to be done now or your bottom will hurt. It's time to do it together so you can go back to playing."

Give them notice
When babies and toddlers are absorbed in the flow of play, it can feel physically uncomfortable to be interrupted. If it's not urgent, warn your child about what's next, such as, "After you've played in the sand pit, we're going inside to change you."

In the long term

Let your child help
Nappy changing starts as something we *do to* babies. Let toddlers help, by crawling or walking to the changing area, choosing and bringing a nappy to you, and fetching the wipes.

Let them stand up
If your child has moved to pull-ups, it may be easier if they stand as you change them, with something to hold onto. Once they have the balance, ask them to squat so you can clean them thoroughly. Change them only in the bathroom, so they associate poo and wee with the toilet.

Reassess
Could resistance be a sign your child is old enough for potty training? Look for other clues, like crouching or hiding when they have a bowel movement, which shows they are aware of the sensations in their bodies before they wee or poo.

Give nappy-free time
Wearing nappies all the time can be uncomfortable and get in the way of crawling and walking. During nappy-free sessions, put down a waterproof play mat and be prepared for accidents. In good weather, take them outside.

SEE RELATED TOPICS
Why does my toddler say no all the time?:
pp.134-135

"WHY DOESN'T MY BABY WANT TO COME OFF THE BREAST"

For your baby, snuggling into your chest to feed is more than just a way to get food. It's a soft, warm place that they associate with feeling safe and calm.

SCENARIO | Even though your child has been trying solid foods for several months, they still cry in the evening for milk before bedtime.

Being fed while cuddled up to your breast is the experience your baby associates with having all their needs for food, warmth, and calm met in one place. It's time with you that engages all their senses, from the touch of your skin to the taste of milk to the sound of your heartbeat. Whether you breast- or bottle-feed, it boosts the circulation of feel-good chemicals in their brain and body. Feeding like this is their earliest memory of life, and the basis for their survival and sense of security, so your baby may not want to give it up yet, even if they are now getting plenty of solid food. To ease this transition, show them that they can always find comfort in your arms, without getting fed there.

WHAT YOU MIGHT BE THINKING

Now they're on solids, aren't they getting too old for this? How long should I keep going?

SEE RELATED TOPICS
Why won't my toddler give up their dummy?: pp.128–129

WHAT THEY MIGHT BE THINKING

- **Your baby may cry** in the evenings if they don't get fed, as they cannot yet separate the experience of being soothed from the experience of getting milk.

- **Your baby may rely on feeding** to go to sleep. Breastfeeding releases soothing oxytocin and contains tryptophan, an amino acid that helps them feel sleepy.

- **If your baby** has not yet learned to drop off by themselves, they may now panic if they are expected to do this without falling asleep at your breast.

- **If your baby is going through changes**, like moving home, being ill, or starting potty training, feeding at your breast is the place where they feel safe again.

> **SHOW THAT THEY CAN ALWAYS FIND COMFORT IN YOUR ARMS.**

HOW YOU COULD RESPOND

In the moment

Redirect
When your child wants to feed from you, turn their attention to something else they enjoy, like a story or song. Give them a cuddle and a kiss that doesn't involve feeding. You may be surprised by how quickly they are distracted by new things if you are consistent.

Offer alternatives
If your child is really hungry or thirsty, offer alternatives. You could say, "It looks like you're thirsty. Shall I get you a lovely drink of water?" As you wean them, keep cheerfully offering alternatives.

Phase it out
If you would like to stop breastfeeding, look at ways to gently reduce feeds, one at a time. Don't refuse them, but don't offer them as often, either. This will naturally reduce your own milk supply and encourage your child to get used to nourishment from other sources.

In the long term

Change your routine
Take a break from the usual routine. For example, if you often feed in the evenings after a bath, or in the morning, ask your co-parent to take over then, to break the habit.

Give other one-on-one closeness
Make sure they get lots of cuddles from you, so they know that your arms are still there to make them feel safe, even if they are not feeding at the same time.

Tune in to your child's pace
If you are weaning too quickly for your child, you may see more tantrums, and clinginess. If so, slow the transition.

Keep it up
There are lots of benefits to breastfeeding into a second year, as it will keep protecting your child against illness. If it's still benefiting one or both of you, carry on, but put boundaries around it – like restricting it to bedtimes.

CHAPTER 3

YOUR 12–18 MONTH-OLD

CREATING A SENSE OF SAFETY

You are your child's world. They depend on you to survive. When their needs for food, warmth, touch, and companionship are met consistently, they start to feel like the world is a safe place.

If these needs are not met regularly – they are left to cry or their distress is ignored – it shapes what a child expects from the world, in childhood and in adulthood. Over time, a lack of safety interrupts their attachment to others, their ideas about who they are and what they can do, and what to expect from future relationships. While it's every parent's instinct to meet their child's needs, modern life, stress, and non-evidence-based parenting advice designed for the convenience of adults can get in the way. Seeing the world from the point of view of your baby can keep you focussed on what they need to develop a sense of emotional security.

1
Smooth the transition
When your baby is born, they go from a warm, safe environment into a cold, confusing one. Try to create sensations of rocking and warmth in their first weeks, to help them adjust.

4
Be there to comfort
Babies come with highly reactive nervous systems. They learn from you how to regulate them. It's not possible to hold a baby too much or to "spoil" them. When you soothe them after they are distressed, this signals to their nervous system that all is well.

> " "
> IT'S NOT POSSIBLE TO HOLD A BABY TOO MUCH OR TO "SPOIL" THEM.

Creating a sense of safety | 111

WORKING THINGS OUT
8 key principles

2
Observe them
By watching your child's facial expressions and body language as they grow, you can identify what they are trying to tell you. You won't get it right every time, but you will help your child feel seen, and important to you.

3
Communicate nonverbally
Long before your baby understands words, they are constantly scanning your facial expression and tone of voice, to see if they are safe. Your child will do the same when they get on the move. Be available – not staring at a screen – so they can read your face.

5
Be their secure base
Allow your baby to gently push their physical capabilities. As they grow into toddlerhood, let them take appropriate risks outside, so they test their bodies to run, jump, and climb. Even if they get the occasional bump, it will help show they can bounce back, making them more resilient.

6
Co-parent on the same page
If you are raising a family with a partner, understand each other's perspectives so you agree on boundaries for your child and apply them consistently. Remember too that children can pick up tension between caregivers. If you are often in conflict address the underlying issues, so your child does not feel frightened.

7
Be aware of what you bring
Look back to your own childhood and see what issues you may be bringing to parenting. These may be ideas about what your child "should" be – or how they "should" behave. Parent your unique child according to who they are.

8
Look after yourself
If you become overwhelmed, it's much more difficult for you to be emotionally available and to attune to your child. Build a village of caregivers for your child, so you are not trying to do it all on your own. See asking for help from others as a sign of strength in your parenting, not failure.

TAILORED ADVICE

Avoid labels
It's easy to brand your child "naughty" or "difficult" if their behaviour is inconvenient. Think instead of your child as struggling with difficult feelings, so they don't feel rejected or unloved.

Create routines
Help the world feel predictable by creating routines, so your child knows roughly what's coming next, whether it's mealtimes, bedtime, or play time. Create routines where things happen in the same order, but are flexible enough to suit your child's development. If you are overly strict, you may stop connecting with your child's needs.

"WAS THAT MY BABY'S FIRST WORD?"

Your baby has been speaking to you for months. But you will probably only identify their first word when they get better at forming it – and you get better at spotting it.

SCENARIO | As your cat walks past, your baby points at it and says, "Caa".

For the last few months, your baby has been making the closest approximation to words they can, given the development of their jaw, mouth, and tongue muscles. With lots of practise, these sounds are getting easier to understand. The first words you spot will probably be things they see or hear often and are made up of simple syllables which are easier to say. This could be Mama, Dada, cat, or dog, as well as social words they hear often, like bye. Listen carefully and you may also notice they are using "That" and "There" (starting with an easier-to-say D sound to make "Dat" and "Der") to direct your attention to things they want you to look at or give them.

WHAT YOU MIGHT BE THINKING

Is that their first word? I am so excited! How many other words are they saying that I don't understand yet?

SEE RELATED TOPICS
How fast is my toddler learning new words?: pp.188–189

WHAT THEY MIGHT BE THINKING

- **Your child has to learn** lots of skills to start to talk. After months of practise, they are now able to form shapes with their mouth to produce recognizable words.

- **Because your toddler** only has a basic repertoire of sounds, they will often use just the first letter of the word to identify what they want, for example "b" for ball.

- **Your child will be thrilled** when you understand them. They will use their first word again and again if you show you understand it and repeat it back to them.

- **Once your child knows** that words are symbols for objects, they will discover that when they say things like "Mi" for milk, you are more likely to take notice.

HOW YOU COULD RESPOND

In the moment

Listen out
The more you listen to your baby's sounds, and look for patterns, the sooner you will recognize what your infant is trying to say. When they repeatedly make the same sounds, as well as point or get excited, look at what they are looking at and name it for them.

Avoid screens
Babies learn best in the real world, so take them out and give them experiences they can name, rather than try to build vocabulary with apps or flashcards. Written words will make little sense to a child this age out of their 3-D context.

Reinforce
To help them understand a word, show it to them real in life – and emphasize it in a sentence. For example, "I see the DOG over there. DOG." A child at this stage needs to hear a word isolated and repeated several times before they add it to their vocabulary.

Avoid comparisons
Many skills go into learning to talk. Unless you notice other delays, avoid comparing how many words they say. Let their vocabulary unfold naturally, without forcing them to say a word you'd like them to say, like "Daddy".

In the long term

Don't rush
Concentrate on naming things so your child builds up a basic vocabulary of nouns. Numbers, colours, and sizes are abstract concepts your child is not yet ready to grasp. Verbs and adjectives also come later.

Let them fill in the gaps
Leave words out of the songs you sing most. Leaving "BOAT" out of "Row, Row, Row the BOAT" gives your child the chance to fill it in.

Put away your phone
If you look down at a screen as you speak to your child, they can't work out the context or the meaning of what you are saying. You also won't pick up what your child is trying to tell you or respond. Over time, this discourages your baby and leads to language delays.

> **" "**
> NAME THINGS SO YOUR CHILD BUILDS UP A VOCABULARY OF NOUNS.

"WHY DOES MY TODDLER LOVE 'LET'S PRETEND' GAMES?"

In their second year, your child will play "Let's Pretend" games as a way to understand and copy what they see in their world. If they invite you into their make-believe world, follow their lead.

SCENARIO | Your toddler is pretending their toy animals are ill and taking their temperature with a spoon, to mimic what you do for them.

In their second year, your child has more refined motor skills to be able to copy the activities they see you do most, like caring for them, making meals, chatting on the phone, or household tasks. "Let's Pretend" play brings a huge range of benefits for your child. It improves their dexterity and hand–eye coordination as they mimic your actions. Through pretend play, your toddler is also learning to be social, as well as working through previous experiences and making sense of them. When you join in, they learn to take turns, which is a key social skill needed for their friendships in future. If you describe what you see happening, you also help your child to learn new words.

WHAT YOU MIGHT BE THINKING

It's so funny to see them copying me. Now I am wondering if I should join in.

SEE RELATED TOPICS
Why does my toddler think their toys are real?: pp.160-161

WHAT THEY MIGHT BE THINKING

● **Your toddler** is creating their own world in which they are in charge. When they invite you in, they will want you to play by their rules as they will enjoy making their own decisions.

● **If you make a few suggestions**, they are learning they have separate thoughts and feelings from you.

● **They expand their imagination** by discovering that an object can represent something else. So, a stick can "be" a thermometer, or a rectangular block can "be" a mobile phone.

● **Your toddler is playing** for the joy of playing. When you join in a game they have dreamed up, they feel valued by you.

"Why does my toddler love 'Let's Pretend' games?" 115

> **THROUGH PRETEND PLAY, YOUR TODDLER IS LEARNING TO BE SOCIAL.**

HOW YOU COULD RESPOND

In the moment

Go with the flow
When a toddler is role-playing, they are choosing to work through their experiences, like pretending to feed their toys or talking on the phone, which they have seen you do. Try not to direct them, take the game over, or "teach".

Be in the moment
Make-believe games can feel repetitive to grown-ups. However, if your child asks you to take part, accept their invitation as far as possible and be patient. If you can, leave your phone in another room. It's a worthwhile investment in your child's development.

Let them make the rules
Toddlers are always being told what to do by grown-ups. If you give your child control over their make-believe world, they are less likely to need to take charge at other times, such as meals or bedtimes.

In the long term

Make it possible
Leave simple props like cardboard boxes or household objects around your home so your child has a lot of opportunities to use them for role-play. Without interrupting, describe their actions. This will make your toddler feel like what they are doing is important.

Give them notice
Your toddler is still building their concentration span, so often it won't be long before they switch to something else. If possible, don't interrupt their flow. If you must interrupt their game, prepare them. Say something like, "After we've put the tiger to bed so she'll feel better in the morning, it will be time for us to start your bath."

Join their play daily
Being available to take part in their playtime every day on a regular basis will help your toddler feel secure in your love and less demanding at other times.

"WHY DOES MY TODDLER MAKE SO MUCH MESS?"

Play, exploration, and curiosity are key to your toddler's development. In order to learn, they have a brain wired for discovery. This can look like opening and emptying every cupboard and container they can get their hands on to see what's inside.

SCENARIO | Now your toddler is mobile, your home feels like a bombsite because they are constantly looking for new things to explore.

Your toddler has a brain designed to seek out new experiences and pay attention to objects they have never seen. As soon as they could point, they directed you to new things. Now they are crawling or walking, they are discovering how good it feels to explore these by themselves. That's because their seeking brain is wired to release the get-up-and-go brain chemical dopamine when they explore – and this makes your toddler feel good. Though it may be more work for you for now, it's worth valuing your toddler's curiosity. It has a huge range of benefits for your child, from improving memory to driving them to learn.

WHAT YOU MIGHT BE THINKING

As fast as I put everything away, they pull everything out. I'm starting to resent the mess. No matter how many times I say no, my child takes no notice.

"Why does my toddler make so much mess?"

WHAT THEY MIGHT BE THINKING

- **Your toddler** can now use both hands together and can push and pull, which gives them the skills they need to open and empty cupboards and containers.

- **Now your child knows that things exist** even when they can't see them, they are fascinated by what's behind doors – and how opening and closing them makes things appear and disappear from view.

- **Your toddler lives in the here and now** and doesn't see untidiness as annoying or stressful. It is more fun, because there's so much to look at on the ground.

- **When your toddler is interested in something** they may go into a flow state of total absorption, due to dopamine helping to boost their concentration skills.

> ❝ ❞
> PLAY, EXPLORATION, AND CURIOSITY ARE KEY TO YOUR TODDLER'S DEVELOPMENT.

HOW YOU COULD RESPOND

In the moment

Encourage exploration
Curiosity is a lifelong asset. Research shows parents have a big influence on how curious their children grow up to be. Rather than be angry or disapproving, share your child's excitement and pride. You can help them learn to be tidy after this phase.

Tell them what they *can* do
Try not to say what they can't do too much. Saying no often will mean they are less likely to pay attention when you *really* mean no. Instead, try to direct your toddler towards what they can do.

Create "yes" spaces
Look at the area where you spend the most time, from your toddler's point of view. Secure any cupboards or objects you don't want them to get into. On a shelf they can reach, rotate a few toys to play with whenever they like.

In the long term

Offer freedom to explore
Saying "don't do that" a lot triggers your child's stress and fear systems, interrupting the release of dopamine and dampening their curiosity. Direct them to what they *can* do instead.

Sing a tidying-up song
Come up with a song that signals to your toddler it's tidying up time for both of you. Make this a fun and predictable part of their day.

Make life easier
The more relaxed you are about mess, the more you will enjoy their exploration. Look for easy clean-up opportunities. Pull down the door of the dishwasher as a tray for their messy play or give them chalks to draw on outside walls, which wash off in the rain.

Take your toddler outside
Nature encourages your child to explore and use their whole body in play – and there's no clean-up afterwards. Whatever the weather, get them outside every day.

Let it go
What your child is learning now will bring lifelong benefits. Encouraging exploration and curiosity means they are more likely to grow into curious and engaged learners.

SEE RELATED TOPICS
Why does my toddler have so much energy?: pp.194-195

MEMORY

Now your toddler is older, you might wonder how much they are remembering. After all, no matter what special experiences we give our child, very few of us have any conscious recollection of events in our lives before the age of around three to four.

This doesn't mean that your child can't remember – they are just busy building on what they learn. They won't remember events like their first birthdays or Christmases, probably because the regions of their brain – like the hippocampus and prefrontal cortex – which govern the processing, storing, and retrieval of episodic memories still have lots of developing to do. It may also be because they don't yet have enough language to help organize their experiences and re-tell them in their minds in a way that makes a long-term memory out of them. Even so, they are storing their emotional experiences of the world, the words they hear, and all the motor skills they are learning, such as walking.

1
Your child's memory is improving all the time
With every month, your child's memory of events in their lives is getting better. Month-old babies can remember events for about a day. By about a year old, they can remember events up to a month later. However, they won't hold onto them in the long term. Even so, they will recognize things that are familiar, like caregivers, and toys and books that belong to them.

> **THEY ARE STORING THEIR EMOTIONAL EXPERIENCES OF THE WORLD.**

WORKING THINGS OUT

6 key principles

2

Repetition helps them learn
Repeating songs and books helps your child build their memory and make new connections in their brain. Avoid forcing it, but try to create a balance so you read and sing familiar books and songs, and introduce your child to new things, to help them learn.

3

They are always building on what they learn
As they rapidly learn the small steps that add up to big milestones, like walking, jumping, and running, your toddler is hardwired to build on their daily progress. This "procedural memory" means that once they learn to ride a bike, they won't forget.

4

Memory is the cause of separation anxiety
Now your toddler's memory is improving, they know you are somewhere else even if they can't see you – which means they start to miss you when you are not with them. Be patient. The phase will pass as their improving memory also helps them to learn that you always come back.

5

Routine helps toddlers feel secure
Repetition helps build your child's memory. Their concept of the passage of time is based on knowing that things happen regularly – getting up, eating meals, and going to bed. When repeated day after day, these routines help your child predict what's going to happen next, which can help them feel secure in their world.

6

Your child stores emotional memories
Even if your toddler has no memory of specific events, giving them consistent care helps them learn that you will meet their needs. This makes the world feel like a safe place now and in the future. On the other hand, if they regularly feel left alone with their distress, it can cause long-term changes to their nervous system and make their brain's alarm system more reactive over time.

TAILORED ADVICE

Ask questions
Research has found that asking children open-ended questions about past events and then adding in extra details as you recall them together helps develop their memory.

Ask how they felt
Your toddler will remember events for longer if you remind them of how they felt. For example, when recalling turning on the merry-go-round, you could ask: "Do you remember laughing when you went around and around?"

Talk about their day
Your child's long-term memory will develop with practise. As you tuck them up in bed, talk to your child about what you did that day. This helps them to process and encode the experiences of the day overnight.

"WHY DOES MY TODDLER ONLY WANT MY PARTNER?"

Now your toddler is able to communicate more clearly, they will start to express more preferences. One of the ways they may try to do this is choosing which parent they do different activities with, like story time.

SCENARIO | Your child insists they only want your co-parent to put them to bed and read them a story.

The reasons toddlers switch between parents vary and can be fleeting. They may prefer the parent who is not at home as much because they seem more exciting – and they may be more likely to give their undivided attention when they get back. Or they may want to stick with the parent who is a familiar part of their established routine and is more engaged at times like bath and story times.

Your toddler may ask for the parent who seems more available during big transitions, such as the birth of a sibling. Most of the time, having a preference is a sign of growing independence. Your child feels confident that you will love them even if they have asked for their other parent.

WHAT YOU MIGHT BE THINKING

Does this mean my child doesn't love me as much? It's hurtful when they cry for my co-parent when I put so much time, love, and effort into caring for them during the day.

WHAT THEY MIGHT BE THINKING

◉ **As your child's memory improves**, they are more able to remember doing things that made them happy. If they had fun with one parent during story time the night before, they may ask for them again.

◉ **Sometimes a toddler's brain may get "stuck"** on a new request. Once they've decided they want your co-parent, they may find it hard to switch gears. If you say no, this may make them more resolute.

◉ **Asking for another parent** may be your toddler's way of testing boundaries in their small world. It's a sign they feel secure enough that you will keep loving them anyway.

◉ **Your toddler** has not yet fully developed "theory of mind" – the ability to understand that you may feel rejected. As you are an all-powerful grown-up, they can't yet imagine that what they do or say could hurt your feelings.

SEE RELATED TOPICS
Memory: pp.118-119,
Separation anxiety: pp.124-125

HOW YOU COULD RESPOND

In the moment

Acknowledge the request
Show you can handle your toddler's request by pausing to breathe and regulate. If your co-parent isn't around, you could say: "I hear you love it when Daddy puts you to bed. I love Daddy too – let's talk about all the things we love about him while I read you a story tonight."

Avoid taking it personally
You may wonder if you've done something wrong, or feel jealous of your co-parent. However, this is a short-lived phase and a sign of your child's growing confidence.

In the long term

Strengthen your bond
If you think your toddler may be asking for their other parent because they have more fun with them – or you have been distracted – set aside daily one-to-one time to play together and build your connection.

Talk to your partner
If you feel rejected, let your partner know how you feel so resentment does not build up. Set aside time for fun family activities together, to create more balance.

Think about your approach
Have you got stuck in a cycle of saying "no" to your child? Check how many times you are saying "no" and remember that a toddler learns best when caregivers notice the positives.

Be a team
Toddlers feel safest when they have a team of carers. If you and your co-parent show you can both meet your child's needs equally, your roles will be more easily interchangeable, with fewer hurt feelings when your child says they don't want you. For example, take turns putting your child to bed.

Remember that it's a phase
This won't last forever. As your child develops an understanding of your feelings, they will want to be fairer.

> **" "**
> **THIS MAY BE A TODDLER'S WAY OF TESTING BOUNDARIES IN THEIR SMALL WORLD.**

"WHY IS MY TODDLER SO FASCINATED BY ANIMALS?"

Toddlers are naturally drawn to animals and their interest can bring an amazing range of benefits, from helping them to develop language skills to learning cause and effect, and building empathy.

SCENARIO | Your toddler keeps following your cat around the house and loves stories about animals.

By the age of four months, research has found that infants are drawn to looking at moving animals over moving objects – and by nine months old, they make excited noises when they see them. Anthropologists believe this fascination is wired into children by evolution. This is because, during humankind's hunter-gatherer days, young humans had to quickly work out which animals were predators. Another reason is that children view animals as "non-human others", who are different from them but have some of the same needs, such as food and shelter. Your toddler may also sense they are higher up the pecking order than the family pet and so treat them like a younger sibling.

WHAT YOU MIGHT BE THINKING

What do they find so fascinating about our cat, who takes no notice of them? And why is my child so obsessed with animals they've never even seen?

SEE RELATED TOPICS
Is my child old enough to have a friend?: pp.156-157

WHAT THEY MIGHT BE THINKING

• **When they are learning** to form words, your child will enjoy copying animal noises, like "Baa" and "Moo", which are often single syllables and easier to say.

• **Children are fascinated** by how similar yet different animals are, and their enviable abilities such as flying and climbing. They will be intrigued by the feel of pets.

• **The name of an animal** may be your child's first word, especially if you have pets and often talk about them.

• **Learning to touch pets gently** and understand their reactions will teach a toddler self-control. Your child will be interested by how what they do makes a pet move closer or further away.

SHOW YOUR CHILD HOW TO PRACTISE KIND AND GENTLE TOUCH.

HOW YOU COULD RESPOND

In the moment

Make sure animals are toddler-trained
Domestic animals can find the erratic movements and energy of toddlers frightening. Give animals time and space to get used to your child. Set out a separate feeding space so pets don't feel under threat from a toddler when they are eating.

Take it slowly
If you are introducing a child to a new animal, take it slowly and show your child how to practise kind and gentle touch. Show them how to look for cues that the animal is happy to be stroked.

Set a good example
Your toddler is looking to you to see how animals should be treated. If you are scared, they will learn to be too. If you treat animals as sentient beings who have emotions, rather than as toys, your toddler will take the same approach.

In the long term

Let them help with care
Allow your toddler to help with feeding, watering, and grooming. Research has found that children who do this tend to be more sensitive and caring towards other people as well. Studies have also found that babies who grow up with dogs are better at reading animals' feelings and are kinder to all animals they come across.

Build interest in the natural world
Children who help care for animals are more likely to feel connected to the natural world. Teach them how to quietly observe animals, like squirrels and birds, in their natural habitat and look and listen for evidence of animals when they are outdoors.

Talk about what animals do
Help build your child's understanding, vocabulary, and sorting skills by observing and talking about what animals like, what they need, and how they help people.

PARENTS' SURVIVAL GUIDE

SEPARATION ANXIETY

To your child, nothing is as special as the love and care you give them. They know your role is to protect them, and they feel safest with you.

It can be a big transition when they first experience being in the world without you, whether it's going to nursery or being left with a babysitter when you go out. For evolutionary reasons, toddlers are wired to be wary of new people, to make sure they are safe. So it's normal for your child to feel unsure about being left with anyone who isn't close family at first until they learn to trust other people.

To make partings easier, work on your relationship with your child at home first. If you respond to your child with warmth and understanding, you become their secure base. This feeling of being loved and valued will build trust in other caregivers too.

1
Be reliable
To help your child go out confidently into the world, be as emotionally available as you can. When you are a reliable carer, who listens to their cues, and shows you are trying to understand, your child learns to believe that when they express their needs, other responsible grown-ups will also look after them.

> "TO MAKE PARTINGS EASIER, WORK ON YOUR RELATIONSHIP WITH YOUR CHILD AT HOME FIRST."

WORKING THINGS OUT

6 key principles

2
Practise short separations
Give your child experience of being left with babysitters you trust. Keep times short to start with. Suggest a fun activity, give a big smile, and leave them to it. Building up social muscles will help your baby learn to feel comfortable without you.

3
Acknowledge their feelings
Take time to connect with your child before you leave them, and name their feelings so they know you understand. Avoid telling them they are making a fuss. Keep it simple. You could say, "I will be back soon. While I am gone, Granny will play with you. I will see you after lunch."

4
Create an invisible connection
Give your toddler something to remind them you are always thinking of them. This could be a drawing of a heart on both your hands or a picture of you they can look at. As toddlers have little understanding of time, you could say, "When I come back after lunch, we can go to the park."

5
Seed emotionally attuned childcare
Prioritize childcare that's an extension of the warm, empathetic care that you give your child. If you are looking for a nursery, check if your child will have a consistent key worker. Are they interested in your child as an individual? Ask about staff turnover too, so you know your child's key worker is likely to stick around.

6
Balance your care
Nowadays parents can work more flexibly, and from home, more than ever before. By sharing childcare between both parents and family, being available as much as possible in these formative years – even if it means earning less for this phase – can be a lifelong investment.

TAILORED ADVICE

Give practise
If your child screams for you not to leave, carry on with your main plan, while acknowledging how they feel. Otherwise, they will learn that if they protest enough, you won't leave.

Role play new situations
Don't just prepare them for the practicalities. Prepare them for what they may feel. Acknowledge that while nursery may feel different and new to them at first, it will give them new and fun things to do.

Play hide and seek and peekaboo
Both these games reinforce the message that even when your child can't see you, you will come back.

Visit first or go early
If you are putting your child into regular childcare, show them their nursery or childminder's home before they go – or in the first week, turn up a little bit early so your child has time to get used to their surroundings before it fills up with other kids. Allow your child plenty of time to adjust and feel safe with any new caregiver.

"WHY DOES MY TODDLER LOVE PRESSING BUTTONS?"

Babies are natural explorers. They are born with an innate drive to discover more about the world and how it works. At times, this will be inconvenient.

SCENARIO | Your toddler is constantly pressing the button on your washing machine and tumble dryer, stopping the laundry from getting done.

Your child's brain is wired for curiosity and to find out how things work through trial and error. Even in their first few weeks, your baby stared at new objects longer than familiar ones.

By now, your child is able to isolate their index finger to point and press. Buttons are one of the most gratifying ways to test cause and effect because when they are pressed, they often make a noise or light up. This gives your child a sense of control over their world and helps them learn how to anticipate events. While it can be annoying, the more inquisitive a child is, the more they learn. Rather than discourage their curiosity, toddler-proof your appliances and find other ways for them to explore.

WHAT YOU MIGHT BE THINKING

Oh no, not again! No matter how many times I tell my child not to, they keep pressing those buttons. I can't get the washing done.

SEE RELATED TOPICS
Why is my toddler fascinated by my phone?: pp.192–193

WHAT THEY MIGHT BE THINKING

• **Your baby arrived in the world helpless.** Now a toddler, they are excited to learn they have some control over events. Buttons are a quick way to test this.

• **Pressing buttons feels good.** Buttons are often designed to feel satisfying to click; your child will enjoy the sensation and seeing what happens next.

• **Your child's vision** has been improving over the last year and now they are more able to focus on finer details, like knobs and controls, in their environment.

• **Pressing buttons to see what happens** activates your child's seeking brain, releasing dopamine, the feel-good hormone of exploration.

HOW YOU COULD RESPOND

In the moment

Avoid disciplining
If it's interrupting household tasks, you understandably want your child to stop, telling them "No!" or pulling their hand away. However, this may make it even more entertaining for them each time they do it.

Childproof important buttons
If they are playing with appliances that are unsafe or inconvenient, such as a dishwasher, try adding childproof button covers or covering them with masking tape until they lose interest.

Redirect them
Offer your toddler toy versions of household appliances or versions of Jack in the Box toys, which pop up when your toddler presses the button, so they can experiment with cause and effect.

In the long term

Show-and-tell
To satisfy your child's curiosity about the washing machine, let them push the buttons under supervision. Next time you do the laundry, ask them to help load it. Then invite them to push the button to start it and show them the results when the cycle is over – wet but clean clothes. The rest of the time, turn the machine off at the socket.

Find other ways to satisfy the urge
Show them how to press the button for the traffic lights, or the button in a lift. Explaining what buttons do will help them learn they have a serious use.

Check your toddler isn't bored
If your toddler is pressing buttons to get a reaction, check they aren't feeling a lack of attention from you. While it's impossible to give them your undivided care, your toddler still wants to feel noticed by you – even if it's just by smiling and acknowledging what they are doing.

> **BUTTONS ARE ONE OF THE MOST GRATIFYING WAYS TO TEST CAUSE AND EFFECT.**

"WHY WON'T MY TODDLER GIVE UP THEIR DUMMY?"

Sucking has a powerful calming effect, which is why many parents give children dummies at bedtimes. As they get older, it can be a hard habit to break without your help.

SCENARIO | A dummy soothed your baby. Now your child is older, they want it during the day, too, and have a tantrum when they lose it.

Sucking on their fingers – and then their thumb – is the first thing a child can do to soothe themselves early in life. You may also have given them a dummy to get them off to sleep. However, it's important that as your child grows, they find other ways to soothe themselves.

If your child has a thumb or dummy in their mouth most of the time, it can hinder speech development. A dummy can prevent babbling, as well as copying words they hear. It can stand in the way of mimicking facial expressions, which they need to communicate. Your child may also get ear infections; a dummy can introduce more bacteria into the throat.

WHAT YOU MIGHT BE THINKING

Giving my toddler a dummy is still useful when I need them to calm down or be quiet. But are they too dependent?

WHAT THEY MIGHT BE THINKING

• **Your child's thumb** or dummy has become a comfort object they have learned to rely on to soothe themselves when you are not with them.

• **Thumb-sucking** and dummies have such a powerful stress-relieving effect that research has found they can reduce pain during injections.

• **If you used a dummy to keep your child calm** and quiet when they are upset, they may have got the message that it's better to push down feelings than experience them.

• **If your toddler has a dummy in their mouth**, it stops them making subtle facial expressions and making the link between these expressions and feelings. As a result, they may find it hard to interpret these cues in others.

HOW YOU COULD RESPOND

In the moment

Think about timing
Have you got in the habit of giving a dummy at certain times, for instance when you are out of the house with other people? Look at what you could do instead.

Ask how your child feels
Help them name how their thumb or dummy makes them feel. You could say, "I see you like sucking on it as it makes you feel happy. Let's think of other ways you can feel happy. How about playing with this toy, or having a cuddle?"

Wind it down
Start phasing the dummy out gradually. Begin with times when they will have other ways to soothe themselves, like story time with you, when you could offer them extra touch. They may go back to using their thumb, but this is often a passing phase.

In the long term

Let them express upset
Parents find it hard to see their child in distress. But children still need an opportunity to cry to let out tension, without getting the message that these feelings need to be fixed or "plugged" with a dummy. Allow their tears to flow to send the message that all feelings are allowed, and let them move through these emotions.

Offer other ways to soothe
Before you take away the dummy, show your toddler different ways to feel calm and safe, like singing to themselves or holding a cuddly toy. Offer praise or small incentives when they choose to stop, such as a sticker when they go for a day without it.

Avoid a rush
Choose a stress-free period to help wean your child off their dummy when you can be around to soothe and offer comfort, as well as distraction, to your child. Expect it to take several weeks or even months.

SEE RELATED TOPICS
Why doesn't my baby want to come off the breast?: pp.106-107

> " "
> **CHOOSE A STRESS-FREE PERIOD TO HELP WEAN YOUR CHILD OFF THEIR DUMMY.**

"WHY WON'T MY TODDLER EAT THEIR DINNER?"

By now, your toddler has got the hang of eating solid foods. As they develop their independence, they may go through a phase of being more selective about what they eat.

SCENARIO | Your child is more interested in playing with food than eating it – and is refusing to open their mouth when you try to feed them.

Your toddler doesn't have much power over what happens to them. However, one choice that is always in their control is what they eat. As food tends to represent love and nurturing in our minds, when a child doesn't eat all their food, we can feel rejected, and fearful they are not getting enough nourishment.

What you may think of as encouraging your child to eat, may be felt by them as pressure. The atmosphere you create at mealtimes makes a big difference. For example, research has found that children eat more vegetables when parents don't make a big fuss about it. If your toddler feels anxious, the less likely they are to feel hungry.

WHAT YOU MIGHT BE THINKING

I thought they liked this food, and now they don't. How will I know if they are getting enough nutrients?

SEE RELATED TOPICS
Introducing solid foods: pp.78–79,
Why does my baby drop food?: pp.94–95

WHAT THEY MIGHT BE THINKING

● **After their first year**, your toddler doesn't grow as fast, so they may feel a bit less hungry. If you are feeding them with the rest of the family, you may be giving them larger portions that look daunting.

● **If your child is left in a highchair** on their own to finish their food, they may feel isolated and trapped. They may show this by throwing food off their tray.

● **If your toddler is full**, they may want to play with the food instead.

● **Children this age** have around 30,000 tastebuds, three times more than adults, so foods can taste much more intense.

HOW YOU COULD RESPOND

In the moment

Help them tap into their cues
Learning to notice for themselves if they are hungry or full is an essential life skill. Ask them questions like, "What's your body telling you?" Making them eat when they don't want to will create a power struggle you can't win.

Make it sociable
Avoid leaving them in their highchair while you get on with other things. They will enjoy mealtimes if you eat with them and keep it fun.

Stay neutral
Even if you're thrilled they are munching on broccoli, keep it to yourself. Avoid describing terms like "fussy eater", which they will hear as a fixed label.

Offer smaller portions
Serve small amounts of each food, around the size of their palms, then offer more when they have finished. Never insist your toddler eats everything in front of them.

Look for signs they are full
It's likely they will have eaten all they want after 20 minutes. If they have stopped eating, take away their plate without comment.

Regulate yourself
Seeing food uneaten can be annoying, but keep emotions out of mealtimes. Toddlers almost always eat the nutrients they need to grow. You only need to be concerned if your child is losing weight, lacking energy, or having trouble swallowing.

In the long term

Avoid all-day grazing
If your toddler is always snacking, they may not learn to recognize their hunger cues. Plan nutritious snacks mid-morning and mid-afternoon, but try not to feed them around the clock.

Let them squidge their food
Your toddler wants to use all their senses to decide what to eat first. When they have passed this phase, food will mainly go into their mouths.

Keep trying
Some toddlers are suspicious of tastes or textures at first. They may need to try a food 15 times before they eat it. Keep offering new kinds, with food you know they eat.

> **" "**
> TODDLERS ALMOST ALWAYS EAT THE NUTRIENTS THEY NEED TO GROW.

PARENTS' SURVIVAL GUIDE

WALKING

Babies start walking at their own pace – and at a wide range of ages from ten months to the middle of their second year, depending on factors like size, strength, and genetics.

First steps are a culmination of many stages of growth and development. At first, babies toddle side to side with their feet far apart and legs straight. Because they are top-heavy, they fall down a lot and find it hard to start and stop. It will take lots more experience before they start to develop a more mature gait with longer, faster, more forward-facing strides.

Be prepared, too: walking may herald a new phase in your relationship. Now your child can move fast in any direction, they will interact with you more, show you things they discover, and look to you for more answers. Once a child is fully mobile, you may struggle to keep up; toddlers can walk an average of 2,368 steps and cover 708 metres (0.44 miles) an hour. Look for ways to offer them freedom of movement without having to say "stop" or "no" all the time.

1
Expect falls
Your toddler has no fear of falling. Expect them to drop to the ground often as they try out their balance. On the first day they walk, research has found toddlers will fall around every five steps. After three months, it's once every 150.

4
Expect a word explosion
Your toddler is now seeing the world from a whole new vantage point. As they will want to point out and get more feedback from you about the new things they see, expect an explosion in the number of words they are using.

WORKING THINGS OUT
6 key principles

2
Give space
Toddlers make the most progress if they can take steps in a row without needing to stop. Consider creating an open area at home, as well as giving your child daily walking time outside, to give them this opportunity. Be aware of furniture they can bump into or pull over now they are mobile.

3
Let them go barefoot
When your toddler starts to walk, they still have flat feet. As they walk, this will be replaced by a muscular arch that allows more precise steps, heel first. Allow them lots of time without socks or tights so they get used to the sensation of putting their weight through their whole foot.

5
Avoid putting them in walkers
Your baby can get more practise by pushing trolleys to help them walk forward. Check safety advice before using baby walkers. These encourage them to walk on tiptoes instead of building the upper leg strength they need. They are also too young to understand the risks of moving so fast.

6
Offer challenges
Your toddler's walking style will evolve quickly over the next four months as they learn to tackle different surfaces, slopes, and getting around obstacles. The more practise they get, the more smoothly they will be able to walk – and move onto the next stage; running.

> **TODDLERS MAKE THE MOST PROGRESS IF THEY CAN TAKE STEPS IN A ROW WITHOUT NEEDING TO STOP.**

TAILORED ADVICE

Let them learn at their own pace
Unless they show no signs of walking by 18 months, just give them opportunities, rather than trying to teach them before they are ready. However late they start, by the age of two most children will be walking at the same level.

Let them go nappy-free
Research has found it's harder for babies to walk when wearing nappies because it makes them waddle with their legs further apart. Offer them nappy-free time – and dress them in clothing that won't restrict their movement.

Avoid hands above head
If you want to support your child, don't hold their hands over their head as you walk them. They need their arms for balance, and to get used to the feeling of their feet landing squarely on the ground. If they feel pulled up by you, they could start to walk on tiptoe. To practise stepping, hold them around their ribcage from behind.

"WHY DOES MY TODDLER SAY **NO** ALL THE TIME?"

Easy to say, and attention-grabbing, "No" is a toddler's first major declaration of independence – and when they first discover its power, they may be excited to use it as much as possible.

SCENARIO | Your toddler has started saying "No!" a lot – and is now refusing to go home from the playground.

Until now your toddler has had all their decisions made for them. Now they have more agency, they want to try making more decisions for themselves. The word "No" is the shortest and easiest way to express their will, and it gets an immediate reaction from you.

Though it can be frustrating, see it as a healthy sign your toddler now sees themselves as a separate person with their own wants. Rather than a battle of wills you have to win, view this as a phase in which they are bravely testing what happens if they don't always do what you want.

WHAT YOU MIGHT BE THINKING

This is exhausting. Why does every little thing turn into a power struggle? Don't I have to nip this in the bud?

SEE RELATED TOPICS
Why won't my toddler eat their dinner?: pp.130-131

WHAT THEY MIGHT BE THINKING

◉ **Your toddler may say no** when they don't mean it. Often, it's the easiest way to express that they don't want to do something. It can also mean "I've had enough", or "not yet".

◉ **If you are inconsistent** about rules like bedtime, your child may experiment with saying "No" to test your boundaries.

◉ **Your toddler is an explorer** who is testing cause and effect. They are testing what happens if they say "No" to the most powerful people they know.

◉ **If your toddler is absorbed in an activity**, for example playing, it may take a lot of mental effort to switch off. "No" may be their way of saying, "I am not ready".

HOW YOU COULD RESPOND

In the moment

Don't be scared of their "No"
Saying no is a natural part of your child's development, and often a way for a toddler to let you know they feel like doing something different. It might be a way to express how they feel, rather than a challenge to your authority.

Don't give "No" power
If you react strongly every time, you will be showing it's a guaranteed way to make you take notice. Pause to regulate yourself before you respond.

Show them you understand
If you summarize what your child is trying to say, they will know they have been heard and be less likely to keep resisting. For example, you could say, "You want to keep playing. But it's time to walk home now."

Hold the bottom line
If refusing is not an option, state your position as a fact, rather than a question. Instead of saying: "Are you ready to go?" tell your child: "After we've finished in the sandpit, we're ready to go."

Be playful
Instead of having a battle of wills, try humour. If they say no to leaving the park and getting in the pram, crouch down to their level. Say something like: "It's time to catch the Choo Choo train home. Would you like to be the driver?" Having a shared goal, and helping them feel important, may dial down their objections.

In the long term

Offer limited choices
Provide more control by giving them two options – both of which would work for you. For example, you could say, "Would you like to pretend to be a train driver or to be a pilot of a plane while we walk home?"

Say no less often
It's easy to slip into the habit of trying to control mobile toddlers with repeated "No's". This quickly teaches them its special power, and encourages them to try it for themselves. Focus instead on saying what you DO want your toddler to do, rather than what you don't. Reserve your biggest "No's" – together with firm eye contact at their level – for important moments.

❝ ❞

YOUR TODDLER NOW SEES THEMSELVES AS A SEPARATE PERSON.

"WHY IS MY TODDLER REFUSING TO GO TO SLEEP?"

All parents know that toddlers are happier and better behaved when they have slept well. However, that doesn't mean your child won't resist going to sleep at bedtime.

SCENARIO | Your toddler now delays bedtime for as long as possible, cries when you leave, and even climbs out of their cot to come and find you.

Now your child wants to exert their will more, they may start fighting bedtimes. One of the main reasons is they don't want to face the next 10–12 hours without you. They are also aware that you are awake elsewhere, and don't want to miss out.

The pain of being separated from you will trigger a rise in their stress hormones. This can turn to crying which is their attempt to get you back so they feel calm and regulated again. As well as checking they are tired enough – from getting enough exercise and not taking too many naps – your role is to teach them, over time, to soothe themselves to sleep.

> **WHAT YOU MIGHT BE THINKING**
>
> **Bedtimes are turning into such a stressful battle.** It means I have no time to connect with my partner and I'm starting to resent my child.

"Why is my toddler refusing to go to sleep?" 137

WHAT THEY MIGHT BE THINKING

- **As your toddler can't tell** how many hours it is until daylight, it can feel like being alone in the dark will never end. When the lights go out, all the familiar things in their room also disappear from sight. They want you there to feel safe again.

- **Your child is wired** to want to be close to you as their protector. Now they have the physical strength to climb out of their cot to find you, they may try it.

- **Even if you tell them to stay** in their bed, they have not yet developed the impulse control to resist that strong urge. They also lack the confidence they can soothe themselves to sleep without you.

- **Your toddler is thinking emotionally**, not logically. They will not hear you giving them "reasons" they "need" to go back to bed.

> **SET ASIDE BEDTIME AS A SPECIAL TIME OF AROUND 40 MINUTES.**

HOW YOU COULD RESPOND

In the moment

Reframe it
Long drawn-out bedtimes can be stressful and it's easy to get frustrated when you are tired. See it as your toddler's attempt to keep their connection with you.

Regulate yourself
If you find yourself raising your voice in frustration, it will make your child even more anxious and wakeful. Take a pause to breathe and regulate.

Tell them you understand
Your toddler is desperate for your help to feel soothed. An important first step is to show you understand how they feel. You could say: "I know you don't want to sleep but it's time for bed. We all need sleep to feel happy."

In the long term

Make it consistent
When your toddler knows each step towards bedtime, they are less likely to try things like asking for more stories. Stick to a certain number. If they ask for more, you could say: "I'd love to read more too. But it's sleep time now. We'll read again tomorrow."

Slowly withdraw your presence
You could first try stroking their face gently as they fall asleep. Then try sitting quietly in the corner of the room, using a soothing voice to sing the same phrase so they realize you are not there to interact. Finally leave the room and tell them you will be back to check on them.

Make bedtime special
Set aside bedtime as a special time of around 40 minutes, long enough for a toddler to start getting sleepy. If you have more than one child, stagger bedtimes to give your youngest child one-on-one attention. Try using humour to help your child like bedtimes more, like helping them tuck in their toys at the end of the bed.

Let them know what will happen
Preparation for bedtime starts during the day. Create a story around bedtime. Ask your toddler what games they would like to play in the bath and which toy they are taking to bed tonight.

SEE RELATED TOPICS
Why does my toddler have so much energy?: pp.194-195

"WHY DOES MY TODDLER HAVE A FAVOURITE TOY?"

Once your child understands that they are a separate individual, it can make them feel alone and frightened. They may want a security object to carry when you are not with them.

SCENARIO | Your toddler takes their toy rabbit everywhere. When you get home from a walk it's missing, and they are inconsolable.

From eight months, your child begins to understand that they are a separate person. To help them cope with their fears about being independent, most children will latch onto a favourite "transitional" object such as a blanket that smells of you or a cuddly toy that becomes special because of its size, feel, and familiarity.

As they branch out into the wider world the object will remind them of you when you are not with them. They also give your toddler the ability to soothe themselves – an important skill. These attachments peak between 18 months and three years, and they become less important as children start to attach more to their peers.

WHAT YOU MIGHT BE THINKING

I can't believe we've dropped my toddler's comfort toy. It was smelly and dirty, but they took it everywhere. How will I get them to sleep now?

SEE RELATED TOPICS
Why does my toddler think their toys are real?: pp.160-161

WHAT THEY MIGHT BE THINKING

- **A comfort object** helps make them feel safe. Research has found that toddlers want them most when they are sad or sleepy.

- **Your child may associate** a comfort blanket with feelings of safety when they were rocked or fed by you. They may reinforce these soothing feelings by sucking their thumb as well.

- **Your toddler will often choose** a comfort toy for themselves. They like that it belongs just to them, and they can do what they like with it.

- **Your toddler may** get attached to a household object – like a utensil, or piece of your clothing – for a while, because it feels like a part of you has rubbed off on it.

" "
SHOW YOU UNDERSTAND HOW THEY FEEL ABOUT LOSING THEIR SPECIAL RABBIT.

HOW YOU COULD RESPOND

In the moment

Acknowledge your child's upset
Show your toddler you understand how they feel about losing their special rabbit – and say you will try and help them find it. If you can't, suggest you help them pick out an alternative to fill the same role.

Regulate yourself
The more anxious you become that your toddler is distressed about losing their favourite toy, the more anxious your child will be. Instead, help your child to develop coping thoughts like, "I miss rabbit, but I can still play with my other toys."

Don't excuse your child's attachment objects
Avoid apologizing for your child's attachment to their toy or blanket, so they know their feelings are natural.

In the long term

See their value
These objects help your child feel safe and regulate their feelings in times or transition, or at bedtimes.

Let them enjoy them
There's no need to wean your child off their favourite object. When this phase has passed, they may still keep their toy in their room, but more as a treasured keepsake.

Double up
If your child takes a comfort toy or blanket everywhere, there's always a chance it will get lost. Consider getting duplicates so you have a substitute. Swap them from time to time so they smell and feel the same.

PARENTS' SURVIVAL GUIDE

TRAVEL

To your child, travelling can feel boring. As soon as they are mobile, they want to keep moving. Sitting for hours restrained by a seatbelt, perhaps away from your touch in the back of a car, can trigger stress chemicals, making them restless and irritable.

Young children don't yet understand the concept of time – or how much longer a journey will last – or legally why they have to be so tightly restrained, adding to their dysregulation. Build in time for breaks to reset their stress levels, and see planning these as an important part of your trip. Reframe the journey as a time to connect with your child, rather than an ordeal to be endured. Remember, too, that travel is a skill that children learn with practise – and exposing them to new places and experiences activates lots of different regions in their brains.

1
Get on the same page as your co-parent
If you are travelling with a co-parent, discuss how you want to plan the journey and how to swap roles. Looking after your own needs, with drinks and healthy snacks, will also help you stay calm and in control.

4
Bear in mind what they can see
After five months old, babies have the depth perception and colour vision to be entertained by looking out of the window. As they enter their second year, you can start pointing out large objects of interest to look out for and you can play I-spy with them.

WORKING THINGS OUT

6 key principles

2
Plan lots of breaks
Sitting in a car seat for long periods is frustrating for your child as it is hard to change position. Map out plenty of rest stops along your route, preferably with green space, or play equipment, and allow time there. If you are flying, rather than boarding early for young families, consider letting them run around as long as possible before you embark.

3
See the journey from their point of view
Is the sun shining on their face through the car window? Does the car seat fit? If it's cold, put their coat over their arms in front of them so they stay warm but have more freedom to move. Take a small light towel to mop up spills, or to use as a blanket on the grass during rest stops. You can also tuck one end into the window and use it to keep out the sun.

5
Check where you're going
When you're driving, it's easy to rely on sat nav to lead the way. But it's helpful to check your route on a map first, in case you miss an instruction with a noisy toddler in the back. Wrong turns will make a long journey longer and more stressful.

6
Talk about the travel rules
Even though your toddler has to legally wear a seatbelt on a car or plane, they won't understand this. To help them do so, role-play your journey and let them hear you tell their toys why it's so important in the days before your trip. This will help your child internalize the rules.

> **MAP OUT PLENTY OF REST STOPS ALONG YOUR ROUTE, WITH PLAY EQUIPMENT.**

TAILORED ADVICE

Take off shoes
Asking an active toddler to keep still for so long is a big ask. If you expect they'll want to spend some energy kicking the back of your seat, take off their shoes.

Pack a potty
For toddlers who are being toilet trained, bring a potty and line it with a nappy you can easily dispose of afterwards.

Avoid giving tech
As tempting as it is, if you give babies and toddlers tech this young, they will not learn to entertain themselves or manage their feelings of boredom. As far as possible, give your attention instead.

"WHY IS MY TODDLER SO **SENSITIVE?**"

Some children are born with more sensitive temperaments, and get overwhelmed more easily. By attuning to their feelings and spotting cues that they are starting to feel dysregulated, you can help them manage their emotions.

SCENARIO | Your toddler bursts into tears every time the tower of blocks they are building collapses.

Around 15–20 per cent of children appear to be born with more sensitive temperaments – also known as sensory processing sensitivity. By toddlerhood, this may show as crying more easily and for longer over things that may not upset other children their age. They may startle more easily and dislike surprises. Big changes – as well as loud noises, bright lights, or strong smells – may also annoy them more. You can help your toddler notice when they are starting to feel overwhelmed and how to calm themselves. Such children thrive when parents understand how the world feels for them.

WHAT YOU MIGHT BE THINKING

It feels like the slightest thing will set my toddler off crying. I worry they will find life difficult if they carry on like this.

SEE RELATED TOPICS
Why does my toddler only want my partner?: pp.120-121

WHAT THEY MIGHT BE THINKING

- **Your toddler may want to control** their environment more to reduce their stress levels, for example by choosing how they like food arranged on their plate.

- **As they seek** to find ways to feel safe and regulated, your toddler may also be more prone to frustration when things don't go as planned.

- **Once they are happy** and in the flow, sensitive toddlers often want to stay in that place. They may struggle to shifting from one activity to another, as it may feel like a painful wrench.

- **Your toddler may cry more quickly** and for longer. They may cling to you when they feel overwhelmed to calm themselves.

HOW YOU COULD RESPOND

In the moment

Help them pause
When they feel overwhelmed, show them how to notice what's happening in their bodies. You could say: "Let's press the pause button", show them how to locate it in their palms, and press their hands together to release tension.

Name the feeling
If your child is about to become upset, you could say: "I can see you're feeling sad about your blocks. Shall we collect them up and build another tower?"

Spot the signs
Tune into the cues your child is getting flooded – like starting to whine, clenching their fists, and fidgeting. Take steps before they get overwhelmed and find it harder to hear you.

Be their secure base
Your toddler may feel bolder about trying new things if they know they can always return to your arms. Rather than view them as "clingy", see it as a sign that they trust you to comfort them.

In the long term

Create a quiet space
Create a chill-out area with grounding objects, such as bubble mix for blowing bubbles to regulate their breathing, or a lava lamp for soothing visuals.

See the upside
Highly sensitive children tend to be more curious, creative, and intuitive. They often have keener observation skills and empathy.

Stay calm
There is a strong genetic connection between sensitive parents and children. Notice when you are feeling frayed or reactive, and take steps to calm yourself. Your toddler is learning from you.

Give unconditional support
Highly sensitive children are more likely to internalize criticism. Use hugs and words of support to show you accept them as they are.

Give new experiences
Help them feel confident about trying new things.

Consider their childcare
Sensitive children may thrive better with one-on-one care, rather than in a busy nursery.

> CHILDREN THRIVE WHEN PARENTS UNDERSTAND HOW THE WORLD FEELS FOR THEM.

"WHY DOES MY TODDLER WANT THE SAME BOOK?"

By reading the same books with your toddler again and again, you are helping them focus and name objects in the world, as well as copy the sounds you make to form words.

SCENARIO | Your toddler is bringing you their favourite picture book to read for the tenth time today.

While it may feel repetitive for you, reading the same story over and over is one of the best ways to boost your child's vocabulary, as well as help them recognize the shape of the words on the page, an essential precursor for reading.

By eight months, for example, babies can recognize specific words up to two weeks after hearing them read repeatedly from a storybook. Toddlers love to read books again and again to practise other skills, like which way up to hold a book, and how to turn pages. Clear static pictures will help your toddler notice, name, and make sense of their world, while the repetition is embedding the words they are learning.

Reading also gives your toddler a chance to talk about the characters' feelings, training the ability to imagine what others think.

WHAT YOU MIGHT BE THINKING

I will scream if I have to read this book one more time. I want my toddler to love books, but I am SO bored!

WHAT THEY MIGHT BE THINKING

● **Your toddler loves** going back to the same book because they delight in knowing what happens next.

● **Your child has your undivided attention** when you read to them, which helps them feel safe, special, and connected to you.

● **Each time you read the book**, it reinforces neural pathways which link sound and meaning in your toddler's brain, building their memory skills.

● **As they turn the pages**, your toddler is learning sequencing – how things happen in order – which will also build their understanding of time.

HOW YOU COULD RESPOND

In the moment

Take it at their pace
Give your child lots of time to engage with each picture. When you go slowly, you give your toddler the chance to copy the sounds you are making and take in what they are seeing.

Shake it up
Rather than read your toddler's stories the same way every time, try telling them in different ways. Give characters funny voices, add actions, or play out the story with their toys. Weave in new descriptive words, like colours and sizes. Share the reading with other caregivers who can offer new interpretations and give stories a new lease of life.

Point and name
Pointing is an important part of reading picture books. Make it a two-way conversation by pinpointing and naming the objects you are interested in. Follow their fingers too, and label what they find interesting.

In the long term

Let them choose
Let your toddler choose their own books. They will find the level that's right for them and move on when they are ready. Offer some small-size books so they can grasp them easily and turn the pages themselves.

Build on their favourites
Books can introduce your toddler to experiences they won't have had in real life, like visiting a jungle. Start with books with realistic, simple illustrations, so they can connect it to what they see in the real world. When you do spot an animal or object they've read about, point it out, to help them make the link.

Keep it fun
Most of all, you want your child to associate reading with fun and closeness with you. Put away your phone. Let your child relax knowing they have your full attention.

Create a reading space
Encourage a love of books by creating a cosy space with a selection of books, on a low shelf they can reach, along with a beanbag or cushions to sit on. The more toddlers are read to, the more they are likely to look at books on their own. Try sitting face-to-face as you read a book, so your toddler can see your expressions.

SEE RELATED TOPICS

How fast is my toddler learning new words?: pp.188-189

"WHY DOES MY TODDLER LOVE TO TAKE RISKS?"

Now your toddler can confidently walk and run, they want to use their newfound skills to explore the world, so they can get frustrated if they feel their freedom is often curtailed.

SCENARIO | Going for a walk is a nerve-wracking experience. Your toddler doesn't want to sit in the pram – and if you let them walk, they run off.

Your toddler is discovering all the exciting ways they can move their bodies – and is exhilarated by the sensation of being able to move faster. Using their body like this also improves their strength, coordination, brain development, and confidence.

However, toddlers are also wired to live in the moment. They are impulsive because the prefrontal cortex, which governs self-control and decision-making, is still in an early stage of development. As relative newcomers to the world, they also lack the life experience to understand what is dangerous for them to do. For now, balance giving them opportunities to move their bodies and explore while showing them how to stay safe.

WHAT YOU MIGHT BE THINKING

My toddler refuses to stay in the buggy, but I can't trust them to walk either because they keep running towards the road. I'm afraid to take them out.

WHAT THEY MIGHT BE THINKING

- **Your toddler is not trying to annoy you.** They enjoy moving faster and more freely.

- **Your child may be excited** if you run after them, and may see it as a game to see how far they can get without you catching them.

- **Though you may not spot it,** toddlers are starting to make risk assessments, although it will take much more experience before they understand what is safe and what is not. In the meantime, they look to you for guidance.

- **"Be careful"** is too vague for a toddler and may make them feel everything is dangerous. If they hear constant "No" and "Don't", your child will stop listening.

SEE RELATED TOPICS
Why does my toddler have so much energy?: pp.194–195

"Why does my toddler love to take risks?" 147

> HELP THEM TEACH THEIR TOYS THE GREEN CROSS CODE, TOO.

HOW YOU COULD RESPOND

In the moment

Talk about it
Before you go, talk about what you would like to happen on your walk. They will understand more than they can speak. You could say, "Pavements are for people. Roads are for cars. We have to take turns." Point out the difference when you are out. Let them know if they run toward the road, it will be a sign they are ready to travel in their buggy instead.

Save your "No's"
Keep your loudest "No" for emergencies. Otherwise keep rules brief and tell them what you do want them to do, not what you don't. "Hold my hand" is simpler for your toddler to understand.

In the long term

Teach the Green Cross Code
Explain simply why people and vehicles have their own places to go because cars are fast and heavy and can hurt people if they hit them. As you hold your toddler's hand to cross the road, engage their seeking brain by asking them to spot the changing symbols and colours on traffic lights. At home, help them teach their toys the Green Cross Code to embed these rules.

Get outside
For millennia, human children were raised mainly outside, and nature is still the best playground. Give your toddler the opportunity every day to run freely.

Offer other fun
If your toddler wants to do what you consider dangerous, like bounce on the sofa, offer alternatives. Rather than forbidding them, you could say: "Sofas are for sitting. We jump on the floor. Shall we sit on the sofa or jump on the floor?"

"WHAT DO MY TODDLER'S SCRIBBLES MEAN?"

Your toddler is eager to start making their mark on the world. Now they can grip a crayon in their fist, and move it around, one way to do that is scribbling.

SCENARIO | Your toddler has been very quiet in the room next door. You discover they have been scribbling on the wall with their crayons.

Improving hand–eye coordination and the fact they can hold a crayon in a palmar grasp means your child can now make their first squiggles.

If you've encouraged them to be creative, they may believe you'll be pleased to see what they have done. There's another reason your child likes drawing on a large surface. They can't yet easily control their crayons and use stiff, up-and-down arm movements, resulting in lots of vertical lines, which are easier to do standing up. These early scribbles will morph into zigzags and swirls – your child's first visual representations of the world.

WHAT YOU MIGHT BE THINKING

What a mess! Where did they get this idea from? Don't they realize it's not allowed? It's so naughty!

"What do my toddler's scribbles mean?" 149

WHAT THEY MIGHT BE THINKING

- **Your toddler is fascinated** by cause and effect – and thrilled that when they put their crayon on a blank surface, colourful lines appear.

- **For now**, your toddler is not trying to "draw" anything and doesn't mind how their marks look. They enjoy the physical sensations and satisfaction of being able to make them.

- **It's easier for your child** to draw with their hand out in front of them than underneath them. They might find it more enjoyable to scribble on a vertical surface than a horizontal one – which may be why they have chosen a wall.

- **A blank wall** looks like an inviting canvas that is not being used for anything else. Having a big expanse is exciting as they don't yet have enough control to make smaller drawings.

HOW YOU COULD RESPOND

In the moment

See it from their perspective
Rather than be angry, be calm and firm. You could say, "I love to see you draw. Walls are not for drawing. Tell me when you want to draw next time and I will find you a big piece of paper."

Let them develop naturally
There's no need to "teach" your toddler to draw. Their scribbles may look random, but any kind of drawing and painting is helping your child strengthen the muscles in their hands and sharpen their hand–eye coordination.

Let them take the lead
Resist the temptation to show them how to draw things, which will dishearten them. Give them freedom to explore.

In the long term

Offer different ways to draw
Buy big rolls of paper to draw on and offer chalk so they can scribble on outside walls. Keep an art basket with washable crayons.

Explore other materials
Young children love to make marks in sand and with sticks in the mud as well as play dough. You could use old toothbrushes or cardboard tubes to make different shapes on paper.

Expand their art
Suggest your toddler lie down so you can draw around them and let them scribble on the outline – or make hand- and footprints.

Encourage expression
Drawing can be an important way for children to express emotion. Start by suggesting they draw along to their favourite song.

Delay screens
When young children are given screens to swipe on, it stops them developing the tripod grip needed to hold a pencil firmly. Give them opportunities to draw instead to develop the hand strength they need for this skill.

SEE RELATED TOPICS
Why does my toddler make so much mess?: pp.116-117

> " "
> **THEY MIGHT FIND IT MORE ENJOYABLE TO SCRIBBLE ON A VERTICAL SURFACE.**

PARENTS' SURVIVAL GUIDE

CHRISTMAS AND BIRTHDAYS

As parents, we often look forward to the joy of giving our babies and toddlers their first birthday and Christmas celebrations, especially if they are our first child.

Children don't have clear memories of events before the age of about three or four. Bear in mind that your own childhood memories of special family events are likely to be based on the years you could remember, usually from around that age, as well as pictures of these occasions. However, even though your child probably won't remember them, marking these milestones is still important. In years to come, looking at photos or videos will help develop your child's sense of their life story and make them feel loved and valued. It's important for you, too. Surveys have found that parents say the best part of Christmas or birthdays is seeing the joy on their child's face.

1
Stick to their schedule
If you decide to throw a birthday party for your child, select a window when your child is at their most alert and even-tempered, often about half an hour after they wake from their regular nap.

4
Put safety first
During celebrations, your home may be filled with new ornaments, candles, and balloons. When decorating, make the transition slowly so your child gets used to the appearance of strange new objects, like Christmas trees, which you may need to childproof as you go.

> "MARK YOUR BABY'S FIRST YEAR BY LOOKING BACK ON HOW MUCH YOU HAVE ALL LEARNT."

WORKING THINGS OUT

8 key principles

2
Keep it small
Too many visitors and lots of fuss can overwhelm younger children. And as parents, we have less time. What your child wants is a parent laughing alongside them, not running around after guests.

3
Match the number of guests to your child's age
Follow the "age plus one" guide. For example, a two-year-old may cope well with three guests, but any more may feel too much. Keep it short too – around one and a half to two hours.

5
Appreciate how far you've all come
There's no obligation to throw a birthday party. Mark your baby's first year by looking back on how much you have all learnt. Expect to feel conflicting emotions of both wanting your child to grow up and stay small.

6
Create memories
Take pictures so you reminisce together in future, and which help children understand their growth. Label the pictures or create a memory book of their first year or Christmas with stories from guests so it becomes a special occasion for them in years to come.

7
See if from their point of view
Avoid too many surprises. Young children can be frightened by loud bangs from party poppers and bursting balloons (which can be a choking hazard). Costumes and party entertainers may also feel scary at this age.

8
Reality check
If your plans for your child's birthday party are getting increasingly lavish, ask yourself where this drive comes from. Are you compensating for a lack in your childhood, or influenced by luxury toddler birthday parties on social media? Keep checking in with yourself: "Is this celebration for me – or my child?"

TAILORED ADVICE

Have a dance
One of the best ways to make a baby or toddler part of their own celebration is to put on their favourite songs. Almost all young children love to move or dance to a beat and guests are likely to want to join in.

Stagger toys
Toddlers play longer with their toys – and use more imagination – when they have fewer of them. So, if your child gets a lot of gifts, hold some back so they can open them gradually.

Take it outside
A young child can be overwhelmed to have so many people in their home. If the weather allows, throw a birthday picnic or play session in the park.

CHAPTER 4

YOUR 18–24 MONTH-OLD

"WHY WON'T MY TODDLER SHARE?"

Your toddler is only just learning about the concept of owning things. Understanding how to take turns and share is an essential skill for the coming years.

SCENARIO | Your child won't share their dinosaur toy with a visiting toddler. When the other child snatches it anyway, your toddler starts to cry.

At this age, toddlers love to share toys and food with caregivers they know. However, they mainly do so to get smiles and positive attention. They are less likely to share with children the same age, because they don't get the same rewards.

Their home is their world, so your toddler believes every toy in it belongs only to them. It will feel like a wrench when another toddler wants to touch their things. These feelings will be amplified if the visiting child takes away your toddler's comfort toy or security blanket. The fear of losing it will trigger anger and tears. Because they don't yet understand the concept of sharing, they will panic in case they never get it back.

WHAT YOU MIGHT BE THINKING

I am angry the other child took the dinosaur, but I also want my child to play nicely. This is so embarrassing.

WHAT THEY MIGHT BE THINKING

- **Your toddler cannot imagine** the world from another's point of view. They do not understand why another child is upset when a toy is taken away, and vice versa.

- **Toddlers live in the moment.** If another child takes their toy, they don't know if they will get it back. All they know is that they were having fun but the toy has gone.

- **Your child is learning** about sharing from seeing you do it. They like sharing with you, as it makes you pleased with them. They don't get the same rewards when sharing with other children.

- **Toddlers this age tend to play alongside** each other rather than together, and clash if they want the same toy.

SEE RELATED TOPICS
Is my child old enough to have a friend?: pp.156–157

> **YOUR TODDLER BELIEVES EVERY TOY IN THEIR HOME BELONGS ONLY TO THEM.**

HOW YOU COULD RESPOND

In the moment

Have realistic expectations
It will take your child several more years to understand how sharing works. In the meantime, don't force sharing. Give your child practise with others their age.

Name what's happening
Acknowledge how your toddler feels and what the other child might be thinking. You could tell your child, "Ben likes your dinosaur and wanted to play with it. Can Ben have a turn? You will get it back before they go home."

Give positive reinforcement
If your toddler is happy to let the other child have a go with their plaything, smile and thank them, so that they are more likely to do it again next time.

Offer other toys
If the dinosaur is not a comfort object, at this age you could distract both children with other interesting toys.

In the long term

Let your child have special things
If another child is coming to play, think about putting your toddler's favourite toys or comfort objects out of sight.

Take them outside
Studies have found that children tend to argue less over objects when they are in nature.

Demonstrate good sharing
When your toddler is watching, ask to borrow something – like a kitchen tool – from your co-parent for a few minutes. Then, return it and thank your co-parent for letting you have a turn.

Play turn-taking games
For example, roll a ball between you so your toddler learns that objects come back even after you have given them to others.

"IS MY CHILD OLD ENOUGH TO HAVE A FRIEND?"

As you responded to their smiles, you have been preparing your child for social relationships since the day they were born, but it will take a while before they make friends with children their age.

SCENARIO | You take your child to visit a friend with a child the same age, hoping they will become friends. However, they ignore each other.

As well as being their parent, you are your child's first friend – because your love and attention shows them how relationships work. By practising the to-and-fro of conversation, you have already shown them how to relate to other people. While this is a critical first stage, toddlers still need to learn more about themselves in relation to others before they are ready to form friendships with children their age. This is because peer friendships take several more skills that need to be practised at home first, such as understanding other people's feelings, imagining what it's like to be them, sharing, and taking turns.

WHAT YOU MIGHT BE THINKING

I was hoping they'd play nicely and be friends, but they are barely taking any notice of one another!

"Is my child old enough to have a friend?"

WHAT THEY MIGHT BE THINKING

- **For now**, your toddler is mainly focussed on winning approval from you, their adult carer, rather than cooperating with other children their age, because that doesn't yet bring the same social rewards.

- **Though your toddler may be curious** about the other child, they don't yet have the understanding or communication skills to interact with each other. Instead of playing together, they are likely to play side by side.

- **Your toddler may show an interest** in the other child by watching or copying the game they are playing. Your toddler is sending the message, "I like the same things as you."

> " PEER FRIENDSHIPS TAKE SEVERAL SKILLS THAT NEED TO BE PRACTISED AT HOME, SUCH AS SHARING.

HOW YOU COULD RESPOND

In the moment

Understand the stage your child is at
Resist the temptation to force friendships. Give them opportunities to socialize with short playdates or toddler groups, so they start getting comfortable around other children.

Help them develop theory of mind
While it's best to leave them to play, you could spend a few moments kneeling beside your toddler, naming what they are both doing, so your child sees the world from the perspective of another.

In the long term

Show your child understanding
If your child trusts they will be treated with kindness and understanding by you, they are more likely to treat others the same way. Chatting to your child, playing with them, and delighting in their company will make them feel liked by you – and likeable to others.

Show them how to imagine what others feel
This ability is an essential component of friendship, which enables key skills like compromise, listening, and sharing. For example, you could say: "Grandma can't visit today because she is feeling ill. That makes her sad not to see you. I am sad too."

Play "let's pretend" games
Pretend play gives children a chance to experiment with social relationships in a safe imaginary space. Research has found that children who play a lot of role-play games are more likely to make and keep friends easily when they get to school. Play games like pat-a-cake to practise turn-taking too.

Model healthy relationships
Your toddler is observing how you engage in relationships all the time. Model basic social skills to others, like saying hello, thank you, and smiling. Role model how you listen to others, regulate yourself during differences of opinion, and take in other people's perspectives.

SEE RELATED TOPICS
Why won't my toddler share?: pp.154-155

"WHY DOES MY TODDLER HATE BEING LEFT AT NURSERY?"

Your toddler is primed to stay close to you. This means that in new situations they may beg you not to leave them with other carers.

SCENARIO | Your toddler screams and clings when you try to hand them over to the staff at their new nursery.

By this age your child knows you continue to exist when you are out of sight. They still protest when you leave, because you are the person who makes them feel most safe and loved in the world.

All children will go through separation anxiety as they learn to be apart from you. Gradually it will pass as they find out they can cope independently. How long this stage lasts can depend on their temperament and how well prepared they are. By showing your child you always come back, and demonstrating confidence in their ability to cope until you return, separations should get easier.

WHAT YOU MIGHT BE THINKING

It's stressful when my toddler screams when I drop them off. By walking away, am I damaging them? I need to go to work.

SEE RELATED TOPICS
Separation anxiety: pp.124-125,
Why is my toddler so sensitive?: pp.142-143

WHAT THEY MIGHT BE THINKING

- **As they see you leave**, your child experiences a sharp rise in stress hormones and will cling to you to try and feel secure again.

- **Your child loves predictability**. They know what to expect when they are cared for by you. They worry their new caregivers can't look after them the same way.

- **Your toddler** hasn't yet built up the life experience to know that when you leave, you always come back.

- **Your child may reject** the new carer just because they are not you and they don't trust them yet. They may react by being hostile or rude to them.

HOW YOU COULD RESPOND

In the moment

Acknowledge feelings
You could say, "You don't want me to go. I see that. I'll be back after you've played with the toys here. I can't wait to see you."

Show faith in your child's carer
Your child is watching your face and body language. Smile, chat, and be friendly to nursery workers to show confidence in them.

Help them look forward
Make your farewell predictable. Say that when you pick them up, you look forward to an activity they know, such as picking up a sibling. As toddlers don't understand time, mention a concrete event like "after lunch". Give your child a ritual like a hug and two kisses, which they know means: "See you later."

Activate their drive to explore
As you walk into the nursery, try helping them to look at any interesting new toys or activities they might want to play with.

Regulate yourself
Your toddler has finely tuned antennae which quickly pick up your emotions. A confident goodbye will assure your child they will be fine without you.

In the long term

Use "brave talk"
Toddlers have separation anxiety because they believe they won't be okay if you leave. Tell them about other times they have coped without you, like being babysat by grandparents.

Take mornings slowly
If mornings are rushed, children are more likely to be stressed when they arrive. Make the journey to school or nursery special time with you, whether it's singing songs or playing games as you walk.

Inform your child's carer
Let the carer know about your child's temperament, likes, and dislikes. Keep an eye on whether the carer seems to be interested as this may indicate how they care for your child when you are not there.

> ## MAKE THE JOURNEY TO SCHOOL OR NURSERY SPECIAL TIME WITH YOU.

"WHY DOES MY TODDLER THINK THEIR TOYS ARE REAL?"

Your child's toys may seem like such an important part of their games that you may wonder if they think the toys are real – especially when they talk to them and bring them everywhere.

SCENARIO | Your toddler insists their toy puppy feeds out of your real dog's bowl. When you find ripped pages in their story book, they blame the toy.

Your toddler now has enough experience of life to act out "let's pretend" games with their toys. This allows them to safely explore boundaries and rules with their playthings. These games are also opportunities for your child to copy what they have learned from watching you, for example that dogs need to be walked and can get into trouble if they destroy things.

However, your child still knows the difference between reality and imagination. For example, they will know that when you make an oink sound for a pig in a book, you are pretending – and imagining – what the real animal sounds like. As their memories improve, around this time your toddler will start to have more vivid dreams, which help them embed memories.

WHAT YOU MIGHT BE THINKING

Does my toddler think their toy dog is real – and do I really have to play along all the time, even when it's inconvenient?

"Why does my toddler think their toys are real?" 161

WHAT THEY MIGHT BE THINKING

- **Until your toddler develops** their first peer friendships, they will use their toy characters as playmates. Playthings do not answer back, and your child gets to decide what happens next.

- **Your child will give their toy** a personality, imagine the care they would need if they were real, and talk on their behalf. This pretend play will help your child develop social skills and imagine the perspectives of others.

- **Your toddler** is increasingly using objects as symbols. As well as giving their toys characters, they may play with a block and pretend it's an apple or a mobile phone.

- **Research shows** that toddlers will now dream about animals more than at any other time of their lives, possibly because like them, they also need the care of adult humans.

HOW YOU COULD RESPOND

In the moment

Play along
Your child already knows their toy puppy is not real. As they develop friendships in years to come, they will naturally start playing "let's pretend" with their peers instead. For now give them freedom to enjoy this phase of fantasy play.

Draw the line where necessary
If your child is sticking their toy's nose into the real dog's bowl, decide where to draw the line. You could say, "That food is for our real dog. Let me give you a bowl of special food for your puppy." Then give them something imaginary so they know you are playing along.

Don't let your toddler blame their toy
Sometimes your child will use make-believe friends as a scapegoat. Use it as an opportunity to state the rules again. You could say, "I'm sorry your puppy has torn your book. Could you please let your puppy know that books are not for ripping? It means we can't read them as easily. They can chew bones instead."

In the long term

Help them develop their imagination
Show you understand their perspective by inventing new things for their toys to do, like grooming their pet puppy. Offer other imaginative play, like making dressing-up clothes available or acting out being characters in your child's books.

Use your child's imagination to help you explain
For example, you could help your child imagine tucking their toys up in bed, as they explain to the toys why sleeping is important for them to feel well. By explaining, they are more likely to internalize the message themselves.

Explain dreams to your toddler
If your child brings up something they saw in their sleep, explain these are dreams – their brains telling them a story when they are asleep. This will help your child tell the difference between scary dreams and reality in the years to come.

SEE RELATED TOPICS
Why does my toddler have a favourite toy?: pp.138-137

INTRODUCING A NEW BABY

The arrival of a new sibling can shake a toddler's sense of safety, especially if, until now, they've had you all to themselves. By introducing the idea gently in the run-up to the birth, they will adjust more easily.

At this age, it's fine to wait to tell your toddler they will have a brother or sister until you have a visible bump. They still live in the here and now, so won't be as excited as you are. Use the run-up to the birth to strengthen both your and your co-parent's bond, with daily screen-free one-on-one time with your toddler. Research is finding that it's not so much the appearance of a rival that throws toddlers off track but the disruption to their routine and having less time with parents. Keep the emphasis on what will stay the same, not what will be different – and let the main message be that there's plenty of love to go around.

1
Offer practise
Role-play what newborns are like with a baby doll. Explain that, at the start, babies mainly sleep, feed, and sometimes cry. Use the doll to practise how to touch the baby softly, too.

4
Show how far they've come
Offer your older child photos of themselves to show how they've grown. Help them feel proud of their progress by saying: "See how the baby loves to look at what you can do."

> " "
> LET THE MAIN MESSAGE BE THAT THERE'S PLENTY OF LOVE TO GO AROUND.

WORKING THINGS OUT
8 key principles

2
Make the intro low-key
A big occasion can feel overwhelming for a toddler. They may sense they are expected to look happy, even when they're not. Consider introducing the new baby in a carrier or held by another family member, so your toddler's first impression won't be that the baby has taken their place in your arms.

3
Allow all feelings
Let them express their feelings, including frustration that they no longer have you all to themselves. If they don't yet have the words, see if they'd like to role-play with toys.

5
Ask for support
This could be asking visitors to pay as much attention to your older child as they did before, rather than just focussing on the new baby, or to look after your new baby for a short time so you can give your toddler your focus.

6
Be prepared for aggression
Research shows your older child is likely to show some anger towards your infant by squeezing or hitting them, although this tendency tends to fall away by four months after birth. Check the baby first rather than directing anger at your toddler, to show they won't get attention by doing this.

7
Decide who needs you most
If both your baby and toddler are crying, avoid automatically tending to your infant's needs first. As toddlers have other ways of communicating, they may need you more in the moment. Make it clear that the baby doesn't always get priority.

8
Expect regression
If young children link being small and helpless to getting more of your attention, they may regress. This could mean more tantrums, wanting to breastfeed again, or going back a step in potty training. Carve out time for them and put off major changes until they've got used to the new arrival.

TAILORED ADVICE

Consider tandem feeding
To build sibling bonding, consider feeding both baby and toddler at the same time, whether by breast or bottle. If your older child has stopped breastfeeding and wants to go back to it like your newborn, explain that your milk was for them when they were tiny, too. Now they are big enough to have snacks the baby can't have. Offer these instead.

Plan story time
In the first few months, when you are feeding your baby in your arms, you could make one session a regular opportunity for story or song time for your toddler.

Free up your hands
In the early months, consider carrying your newborn in a sling to have your hands free for your older child.

"WHY DOES MY TODDLER HATE GOING IN THE PRAM?"

Sometimes you have to get your child on the move. But if your toddler doesn't understand – or agree with – your reasons for putting them in their pram, they may physically resist.

SCENARIO | Your toddler arches their back and thrashes about when you try to put them in their buggy.

Your toddler is full of curiosity and energy and loves to run around freely. While you know the reason why you have to get to your destination on time, your child has different priorities. And just as it would be for us, being restrained can feel frustrating and physically stressful.

At the same time, your child is discovering they have the strength to resist. They may fight an attempt to force them into a position by holding their body rigid or arching their back and thrashing about. By letting them know you understand, you can help your toddler become more cooperative.

WHAT YOU MIGHT BE THINKING

I don't have time to let my toddler walk to nursery today. As they won't budge, and I am running out of time, how do I get them in the pram?

SEE RELATED TOPICS
Why does my toddler keep stopping on our walks?: pp.174–175

WHAT THEY MIGHT BE THINKING

• **Your toddler is fizzing with energy**, which helps them to learn and explore. Strapped in, they are unable to find out about things that interest them.

• **If you are late**, your child will pick up on your anxiety. They may respond by becoming stressed and impatient.

• **Just like adults**, toddlers don't like being strapped in one place, or unable to move, but they have even less control.

• **If your child** is in a forward-facing pram, they can't see your face, and it may be harder to hear your voice and interact with you. They may feel lonely and bored.

HOW YOU COULD RESPOND

In the moment

Let them know you understand
You could say, "I know you want to walk. But it's time to get in the pram so we can get to nursery." If they sit at the start of the journey, they could walk a part of the way.

Give them something to hold
Holding a useful object will give your child something to focus on. It may also help divert them from the experience of being strapped in.

Build in extra time
If the pram is becoming a flashpoint, build in extra time to give them a chance to walk part of the way, or let them have a run around first. When you are not rushed, you are more likely to stay calm, as will your child.

Pick up your child firmly but affectionately
When you have no choice but to get your child ready to go, tell them: "I understand this is hard for you today. Let's chat about what we see on the way." Let your child know that you acknowledge their frustration, but stay in charge.

In the long term

Offer a basic framework
Explain what will happen before, during, and after your journey. For instance, "After you've had a run around, you are going in your pram. We will play 'I spy' on the way. On our way back, you can walk."

Get them seeking
If they can't see you, talk, sing songs, and ask questions so they enjoy the time to connect with you. Ask them to look out for objects. Make it fun by pretending it's a race – with a toy steering wheel so they can feel like they are in the "driving seat".

Look at alternatives
Your toddler might be ready for other ways to get on the move which give them more autonomy, like a push-along bike. Or you could let them stand on a buggy board attached between you and the pram.

Adjust the pram
Now your child is older, they may prefer to sit at a different height and angle. When you are both calm, ask them to sit in the buggy so you could adjust it to be more comfortable.

> **YOUR TODDLER MIGHT BE READY FOR OTHER WAYS TO GET ON THE MOVE WHICH GIVE THEM MORE AUTONOMY, LIKE A PUSH-ALONG BIKE.**

"WHY IS MY TODDLER SO JEALOUS?"

Your child may have looked happy when they were introduced to their new sibling, but is likely to feel jealous now they realize the baby is here to stay.

SCENARIO | You can't leave your newborn alone in case your toddler acts out their jealousy by pinching or hitting them.

Jealousy stems from a child's instinct to get enough food and protection to survive. Firstborns may find it particularly hard to adapt, because they have always had your exclusive attention.

Your child is not only likely to be angry with the new baby. They may also feel confused and betrayed by you for bringing a rival into their home and disrupting their routine. If they've been told how exciting it is for them to have a new playmate, they may also feel disappointed when the only things the new baby does is eat, sleep, and be held by you. If you repeatedly show that life won't change as much as they feared, your toddler's feelings will pass.

WHAT YOU MIGHT BE THINKING

I thought my toddler would be proud to become a big sibling, but they aren't. Plus, they seem so big I worry the baby will get hurt.

SEE RELATED TOPICS
Why is my toddler so sensitive?: pp.142-143,
Why won't my toddler share?: pp.154-155

WHAT THEY MIGHT BE THINKING

- **After the shock** of realizing the baby is here to stay, your toddler is panicking there won't be enough love for them. It's easier for them to take these feelings out on the helpless baby than you, as you are their protector.

- **Your toddler hasn't got the perspective** to realize you have enough love for all your children and your baby won't need your constant attention forever.

- **Depending on temperament**, your toddler may regress by crying more, so you have no choice but to meet their needs.

- **They don't have words** to deal with complex feelings of sadness; it comes out as hitting.

HOW YOU COULD RESPOND

In the moment

Give extra reassurance
If you punish, shout, or banish your older child for hitting the baby, it will confirm their worst fears that they are no longer wanted. See their behaviour as worry that you won't love them as much, and offer reassurance.

Help them name it
If your toddler feels understood, they are less likely to take out their jealousy on the baby. You could say, "I can see that you want the baby to go away," or, "I bet you wish we could play together on our own."

Make it clear you will continue to meet their needs too
Let your child know that you still see their needs and both have to take turns. You could say, "For now, my hands are busy feeding the baby. As soon as I am done, I will play a game with you."

Show kind touch
Your toddler is still learning their strength. Guide them by showing how they can stroke and touch the baby and how they – and you – respond positively.

In the long term

Talk about the world from the baby's point of view
Refer to your arrival by their name, so your toddler learns to think of them as a person. Point out when the baby's interested in what they are doing: "Look at how Noah looks at you. They think you are so clever."

Give regular one-on-one time
Toddlers measure love by the amount of time you spend with them. Find daily time with your older child when your baby is asleep, which they can look forward to. If you have a co-parent, share the baby care as equally as possible, so your toddler doesn't feel one parent has been "taken" from them.

Find other outlets
You could help your toddler safely express their feelings by role-playing a doll getting a younger sibling, or reading books about jealousy.

> ❝ ❞
> **FIRSTBORNS MAY FIND IT PARTICULARLY HARD TO ADAPT, BECAUSE THEY HAVE ALWAYS HAD YOUR EXCLUSIVE ATTENTION.**

"DOES MY TODDLER UNDERSTAND **HOW I FEEL?**"

You may be surprised the first time your child tries to comfort you when you're sad. Welcome it as a sign they have developed empathy – a lifelong skill.

SCENARIO | When your toddler sees you shedding a few tears over a news item, they offer to kiss you better and give you their biscuit.

While it's not as visible as learning to walk and talk, empathy is an essential life skill for your child. At birth, your baby is hardwired to learn to attune to the emotions of others; even very young infants start to cry if they hear other infants cry.

As they grow, your child constantly scans your face to read your expression, as a way to connect with you. With experience, they realize that when they are upset or frightened, they feel better when you try to understand what is distressing them and you give them comfort. In their second year, your child increasingly understands that you have your own separate thoughts and feelings. Now when they see you upset, they want to comfort you back.

WHAT YOU MIGHT BE THINKING

How does my toddler understand what I am feeling?
I hope they are not upset by seeing me cry.

WHAT THEY MIGHT BE THINKING

● **Your child is now old enough** to understand that you have emotions as well as them, and these can be triggered by external events.

● **For now, your child will mainly show care** and empathy towards you and their closest caregivers, rather than people they don't know as well, because you have comforted them in the past and they are more tuned into changes in your emotions.

● **Your toddler has learned** that when they show kindness, you are likely to reward them with smiles and warm words back, which makes them feel good.

> " "
>
> ONE OF THE BEST WAYS TO TEACH EMPATHY IS TO NOTICE AND NAME YOUR OWN FEELINGS.

SEE RELATED TOPICS
Why does my toddler only want my partner?: pp.120-121

HOW YOU COULD RESPOND

In the moment

Name how you feel
One of the best ways to teach empathy is to notice and name your own feelings. When your toddler notices you are crying, they will understand what sadness can look like and all emotions are allowed. You could say, "I saw a very sad story on the news today. It made me cry."

Help your child name their feelings
Mirror back and suggest words for what your child might be feeling. Your child will appreciate the fact that you are trying, and it will help broaden your child's feeling vocabulary.

Offer comfort
Be responsive to your child's distress, rather than telling them to stop crying. By being heard, your child learns to regulate their own feelings and to do the same for others.

In the long term

Make it clear all feelings are allowed
While you feel uncomfortable seeing feelings like anger or jealousy in your child, avoid shaming them or telling how they "should" or "should not" feel. When they learn to acknowledge emotions, they can work through them, instead of suppressing them or turning them inwards.

Use pretend play
Toddlers can learn to think of other people's perspectives using their toys. You could pretend their teddy has hurt its paw and say, "Bear is crying because his paw hurts. What could we do to make it feel better?" Ask how your child would help if someone hurt teddy's feelings. This will show them that painful emotions can be soothed.

Read books with them
This is proven to help teach your child to understand others. As you read with them, ask your child questions and chat about what the characters might be feeling.

"WHY DOES MY TODDLER BITE AND HIT?"

If your toddler uses aggression against other children, it can be upsetting and embarrassing. However, with your help, they will grow out of it.

SCENARIO | Your toddler bit another child who snatched a toy they were playing with. They also hit you when you carry them upstairs to bed.

If your child bites or hits in public, you may feel embarrassed because you fear it will be seen as a sign they are "badly behaved". At home, you wonder why the child you love so much would hurt you. And while it's important to set a clear boundary as soon as it happens, it's also key to understand what leads up to these moments, in the context of your child's development.

Your toddler is still developing control of their body faster than they are learning to express their feelings. Using their body is still the most direct way of communicating, "I don't like you doing that." By showing them better ways to express how they feel, you can help your child develop healthier ways of dealing with angry feelings.

WHAT YOU MIGHT BE THINKING

Am I a terrible parent if my toddler is resorting to violence? Is there something wrong with them? How can I stop it?

WHAT THEY MIGHT BE THINKING

• **If your toddler feels** under threat, it will send them into fight mode. As they don't have enough words to express themselves, biting or hitting may be how they try to "defend" themselves.

• **Your child is learning** that they get a loud and immediate reaction when they bite – so for now, they may be experimenting to see what happens.

• **Your child is still developing "theory of mind"**, or the ability to see the world from others' points of view. They don't yet consider whether biting or hitting hurts someone else.

• **At this age**, other children the same age often feel unpredictable and hard to read. Your child may bite or hit as a wordless way to assert dominance in a war over a toy. It may also be used as a way of getting other children to give them more space.

HOW YOU COULD RESPOND

In the moment

Take a pause
Your child is already in a fight-or-flight state, which is why they bit, and unlikely to hear much of what you have to say. First check the other child is not hurt and offer an apology. Then move your child away.

Regulate yourself
While it's tempting to tell your child off loudly to shock your child into never doing it again, instead take a deep breath, and evaluate the situation.

Say what they should have done
When your child is able to hear you again, get down to their level. You could say, "I saw how cross you got when Lucas took your toy. It's OK to say you didn't like it. But not with biting. Use your words."

See it in context
Behaviour is communication. Your child does not want to make you look bad. They are learning to regulate their emotions. Biting and hitting is a normal part of their development.

In the long term

Embed the rules
Read books about biting and hitting for children their age, with different perspectives on why it's wrong. Make up mantras together like: "Teeth are for eating, not biting" or "Hands are not for hitting".

Offer a re-do
If your toddler feels like it, play out what they could have done differently, with their toys. By explaining to their playthings, they are more likely to internalize the social rules for themselves.

Look for warning signs
Young children tend to clench their bodies, especially their teeth, and their fists before they bite. Help them notice these body sensations in themselves as a sign they need to self-calm, or seek regulation from you. Check for signs of tiredness and hunger too.

SEE RELATED TOPICS
Why is my toddler so sensitive?: pp.142-143,
Tantrums: pp.172-173

> " **IF YOUR TODDLER FEELS UNDER THREAT, IT WILL SEND THEM INTO FIGHT MODE.**

PARENTS' SURVIVAL GUIDE

TANTRUMS

Tantrums are a normal part of a child's development and happen more often in their second year. Your child is becoming more independent and learning through trial and error how to manage their emotions.

They are usually triggered by your toddler feeling overwhelmed, disappointed, or powerless – all common feelings for small children who don't yet have words for how they feel. A toddler screaming because they don't want to go in their pushchair or wear their blue shoes today doesn't yet have the perspective to understand these are minor disappointments that will pass. In the moment, they are experiencing feelings of loss, and also being flooded with stress hormones.

Although tantrums will always happen, parents can help them to pass sooner by providing reassurance, staying regulated themselves, and seeing them as a form of distress – not defiance.

1
See it from your child's point of view
Your child doesn't like having a tantrum. They want to feel back in control. Tantrums are a necessary phase of development, in which children learn to calm themselves.

4
Be there to regulate
If your toddler's emotions are out of control, offer physical touch like a hug or staying close by. Use as few words as possible as your child won't be able to register what you are saying. Don't tell your child to be quiet or stop, so their tantrum is not rewarded with more attention. Avert your gaze, if necessary. Instead stick to reassuring phrases like, "I'm here".

WORKING THINGS OUT
8 key principles

2
Say yes more
Often toddlers want to make more of their own choices. Offer simple alternatives like choosing a ball to take to the park. If a tantrum is over something necessary, like getting ready for bed, stick with your intention so they don't learn it's a way to avoid doing things.

3
Watch for the cues
Look out for cues your child is starting to become dysregulated, like rubbing their eyes, or getting frustrated with a toy, so you can head them off. Common triggers are tiredness, hunger, frustration, and parental stress. Look out too for transition times, when they are switching between activities.

5
Regulate yourself
Research has found that few tantrums last more than 15 minutes. View a tantrum as a cloud flying overhead, telling yourself something like, "This will pass."

6
Say no to hitting
Put them down if they are biting or hitting so you are not at risk. Afterwards, let them know you understand they were frustrated but hurting others never helps.

7
Reconnect after
When their emotions have settled, help them find the words for what happened, like "I see you were cross we had to go in the car." If they have the words, state that the next time they could say: "Tired", "Hungry", or "Need you".

8
Create routines
Have a predictable schedule for sleeping, playing, and mealtimes. If a child is hungry their body will release stress hormones, which will make them more reactive. Being tired and over-stimulated will also make them more prone to explosions.

TAILORED ADVICE

Keep track
If they are having two or three tantrums daily or they regularly last more than 25 minutes, your child is hurting themselves, or you are finding it hard to stay in control, seek advice from your doctor or health visitor.

Take it out of public view
If your child is having a meltdown in a public place, your own brain will go into fight-or-flight mode. Try focusing entirely on your child in the moment, or gently removing them from public view.

Show them their feelings
Help them visualize their emotions passing by shaking up a glitter snow globe. Sit with them as you watch the glitter settle. Help them learn to take deep breaths by blowing out their feelings as bubbles and seeing them fly away.

"WHY DOES MY TODDLER KEEP STOPPING ON OUR WALKS?"

Now your child is walking confidently outside, they will enjoy being able to explore the world out of your arms for the first time. They may find something new and exciting every few steps.

SCENARIO | On the way to a toddler music class, your child insists on getting out of the pram to inspect interesting sticks and stones on the ground.

Your child is building up connections between their brain cells at a speed of a thousand per second, a rate never to be repeated. They make the most of this cognitive development by noticing everything. Furthermore, while their logic and sense of time are still developing, their brain power is focusing in the moment. This means that if you ask your toddler to hurry up, they find it hard to hear you as it takes a lot of brain power to switch attention.

At the same time, your toddler now has the core strength to squat down to look at things on the ground, which is unlikely to be comfortable for you.

WHAT YOU MIGHT BE THINKING

It takes ages to get anywhere because they want to stop to look at everything on the way. I can feel myself getting impatient and now we're late!

SEE RELATED TOPICS
Walking: pp.132-133

WHAT THEY MIGHT BE THINKING

● **Your toddler is engaging** their "seeking" brain, which activates dopamine in their reward system. Humans are natural gatherers, so your toddler is doing what we have always done to learn life skills.

● **Your toddler sees everything** as if for the first time and is trying to figure out how the world works. They have no concept of time, so do not feel you need to rush.

● **When your toddler is absorbed**, their brain shuts out anything that's not directly related to their activity. Even if they hear you telling them to come along, they may not register what you are saying.

● **The texture, colour, and weight** of their discoveries are fascinating to your toddler, and they can now see in full colour.

HOW YOU COULD RESPOND

In the moment

Get down to their level
Instead of pressing your child to hurry up, let them show you what they have found and try to see what makes it so fascinating.

Enjoy the journey
Share your child's wonder at the world. Think of taking your toddler for a walk as an activity in itself, not a means to get somewhere. Try to fit in a daily walk at their pace.

Give them warning
If you've given them time to explore and you need to move on, give them a minute's notice. Suggest they take their stick with them to examine – or take a picture so you can talk about it later.

In the long term

Join them
Enjoy your toddler's discovery of the world. Try doing what they naturally do – walking slowly, looking around, and paying attention to sounds and smells around you. Adopting this approach on walks with your child will help you both feel happier. When you do, try to interrupt as little as possible.

Build in buffer time
Children learn best when they are not hurried and can follow their own interests. To stay connected, aim to do less, too. The more time pressure you put yourself under to get to places, the more difficult it will be to enter into your child's world.

Take your toddler outside more
The outdoors is the best place for young children to practise their newfound physical skills. It allows them freedom to run and jump, be boisterous and messy, and feel adventurous. Offer lots of time for them to explore without a rush.

> **THE OUTDOORS IS THE BEST PLACE FOR YOUNG CHILDREN TO PRACTISE THEIR NEW-FOUND PHYSICAL SKILLS.**

"WHY WON'T MY TODDLER WEAR THEIR COAT?"

Your child is starting to want more independence, and will feel powerful when they can make their own decisions about what to wear.

SCENARIO | It's cold outside but your toddler starts kicking and screaming when you try to put on their coat.

Avoid seeing your child's refusal to wear a coat as a threat to your authority. You are always the all-powerful grown-up. Instead, view this as a necessary stage your toddler needs to go through as they try out new ways to express their wishes.

Your role now is to stay calm, get curious, and show you are on the same team. You wouldn't like to be forced to wear something you didn't like; your toddler can have these feelings too. They just don't have the words to do much about it. They are using their bodies to communicate.

WHAT YOU MIGHT BE THINKING

Leaving home is difficult enough already without my toddler being so stubborn. Plus, it's freezing. I have to make them wear something warm, even if they don't want to!

WHAT THEY MIGHT BE THINKING

- **Your toddler is rejoicing** in their newfound freedom to walk and even run. When they get bundled up, the limits on their movement can feel uncomfortable, especially when strapped into a buggy or car seat.

- **Children love routines.** If you are doing things in a different order this morning, or are rushing them, they may be reacting. It may not be about the coat but just a feeling of not wanting to do something – or resistance to feeling pressured.

- **Young children don't feel the cold as much as adults.** This is because they have a smaller skin surface area to keep warm, they are more active, and have a faster metabolism.

- **Toddlers may find some fabrics are itchy** on their skin, especially children with a more sensitive temperament.

HOW YOU COULD RESPOND

In the moment

Acknowledge their feelings
Get down on their level and speak softly. Tell your child: "I see this is hard today. I can help you decide what to wear outside if you like." By showing them you are taking their objections seriously, you are more likely to calm them.

Step back a moment
If you are losing your temper, remember this moment will pass. The more tension your child feels, the more likely they are to resist.

Offer choice
Offer a simple choice of another coat or a warm hoodie that might be looser and more comfortable. This will help them feel heard.

Let your toddler learn the consequences
If it's not so cold it's a health hazard, allow your child to learn how it feels to go out without a coat. Take a jumper to give them if they change their mind. A scarf and hat may be all they need.

In the long term

Get curious
If this is a common occurrence, work out what might be the issue. Does their coat feel scratchy? Is it so padded, they can't move? Is this really about the fact that you are dropping them off at daycare?

Give your child more time
Is your child feeling rushed by you? During this phase, allow more time for leaving home and make the process more upbeat. Try making up a "We're going out" song.

Let them choose comfier clothes
Allow them to try a new coat on first to check if it feels comfortable. Or use second-hand clothes that have been washed a lot, so they are softer. Cut out scratchy tags. Try looser options which are easier to put on, like a poncho, which you can slip over their head.

SEE RELATED TOPICS
Why does my toddler say no all the time?:
pp.134-135

> "IF THIS IS A COMMON OCCURRENCE, WORK OUT WHAT MIGHT BE THE ISSUE."

"WHY DOES MY TODDLER HATE BRUSHING THEIR TEETH?"

As toddlers realize they have the power to say no, they may start to resist doing things they did previously, especially if they've had a scary experience.

SCENARIO | Your toddler has started clamping their jaw shut when you try to clean their teeth, and becomes hysterical when you try to wash their hair.

When it comes to hair-washing and teeth-brushing, you probably feel firm boundaries will make sure your child gets into good habits. This means these jobs can turn into a battle of wills with parents who feel they have to show their toddler who's the boss.

Listen to your language. If you are referring to your toddler in terms of a battle or struggle, take note. Most children want to be cooperative, so your child is trying to communicate through their behaviour, as they don't yet have all the words. By working with your toddler to listen to their reasons why they don't want to wash their hair or brush their teeth – and working with them to make them feel less scared – their resistance will pass more quickly.

WHAT YOU MIGHT BE THINKING

I need to keep my toddler clean. I don't want to turn it into a battle, but what else can I do, as these things aren't optional.

SEE RELATED TOPICS
Why does my toddler say no all the time?: pp.134–135

WHAT THEY MIGHT BE THINKING

- **If they've had a moment** that frightened them, like getting water in their eyes during a hair wash, they may become more resistant to these experiences.

- **Having an object forced** into their mouths to clean their teeth can feel invasive to your toddler, especially when they don't understand why it's necessary.

- **Toddlers may try to link experiences,** but draw the wrong conclusion. For example, they see the water disappearing down the plughole in the bath and assume it could suck them down too, making them afraid to close their eyes during their hair wash.

"Why does my toddler hate brushing their teeth?" 179

> **TALK ABOUT HOW WHITE AND SHINY THEIR TEETH WILL BE.**

HOW YOU COULD RESPOND

In the moment

Address their fears
At neutral times, ask your toddler what's worrying them. For example, if they are worried about disappearing down the plughole when you bath them, show them how the bath toys won't go down there, so they can't either.

Help them look ahead to the outcome
Talk about how white and shiny their teeth will be and show them in the mirror, so they enjoy the results.

Be flexible
To get your child comfortable with the process, you can use a finger toothbrush made of soft silicone. You could also let your toddler pick out a toothbrush and try tooth brushing for themselves.

Do it alongside them
Your toddler loves to copy you. Clean your teeth alongside them and suggest taking turns.

In the long term

Introduce some fun
Wash their hair by lathering up bubbles to make them a funny shaped hat, which you show them in the mirror. A hair wash or tooth brushing song may help to remind them that it won't last long. Make toothbrushing a game by pretending that each of their teeth is an animal who needs to be "tickled" by the toothbrush.

Understand this is a phase
Parents often worry that if their child won't brush their teeth now, they never will. Remember it's a phase – meet your toddler where they are.

Take it slower
If you are rushing to brush their teeth, your stress may feel contagious, and your toddler may express this through resistance. Let them sit on your lap and try it at a gentler pace.

"HOW DOES MY TODDLER SEE COLOURS?"

When your baby was born, their world looked blurry and in lots of shades of grey. By their second year, your child can see the world in all its colours, even if they don't yet know the words for them.

SCENARIO | When you ask your toddler to bring you their red cup, they bring their blue one instead.

Your child's ability to see colour has been moving rapidly. When they were born, the photoreceptor rod cells – at the back of the retina of their eyes, which enable us to see in the dark and mainly pick up shades of grey – were the most mature. The three types of cone cells, which pick up the main wavelengths of light interpreted by the brain as red, green, and blue, were much less developed.

This meant that, at first, your child's world mainly looked monochrome. As the colour-detecting cones in their eyes developed after birth, and the neural circuitry in their visual cortex started to wire up, their colour perception improved. Within a few weeks, this meant they could see red, green, and then blue in the world around them. Since then, their colour perception has kept getting better.

WHAT YOU MIGHT BE THINKING

After seeing the world in black and white, does my child now see the world in full colour like I do? Why don't they seem to know the names?

"How does my toddler see colours?" 181

WHAT THEY MIGHT BE THINKING

◉ **Even though your toddler can now see all the different hues**, colour is an abstract concept for them to grasp, and they will take longer to label and name them.

◉ **By now your toddler will have an idea of what colour** simple objects should be, for example both a strawberry and a cherry should be red.

◉ **While they can clearly tell the difference between primary colours**, like red and blue, they are not ready to tell the difference between more subtle shades of primary colours, say red and fuchsia.

◉ **Colour words are adjectives**, which are among the last for toddlers to pick up after the two main building blocks of nouns and verbs.

HOW YOU COULD RESPOND

In the moment

Be patient
Your toddler will be able to understand colour words before they can use them accurately in speech. Allow them time to learn nouns and verbs first. If you weave colour words into your language, their naming of colours will come naturally.

One colour at a time
Concentrate first on naming the primary colours of red, blue, and green, before moving on to the secondary shades, like purple or orange.

Try sorting colours
Your toddler is learning to categorize objects by shape and colour. Help them practise this skill by showing them how to pick all the red blocks or blue objects out of their toys. Keep it as a fun game, not a test.

Be specific
To help make it clear that colours are ways to describe objects, instead of saying, "That's red, isn't it?", try "Do you see the red block? Shall we build a tower out of the red blocks?"

In the long term

Show contrasts
As your child's colour understanding develops, you could also offer a choice between different colours. You could say, "Would you like to wear your blue T-shirt or red T-shirt today?"

Keep an eye out
Regular eye tests are essential as any eyesight difficulties can make it harder for children to read and concentrate. As they get older, if they find it hard to tell the difference between basic hues like red, greens, and browns, they may need a test for colour blindness.

SEE RELATED TOPICS
What can my baby see?: pp.26-27

> **WITHIN A FEW WEEKS, THEY COULD SEE RED, GREEN, AND THEN BLUE.**

PARENTS' SURVIVAL GUIDE

POTTY TRAINING

Small children start life never having to think about when they need to wee or poo. So it can feel annoying to interrupt their playtime several times a day to take themselves off to use the potty.

What's more, when they produce the wee and poo that grown-ups ask for, they see it flushed away immediately. Give some careful thought to what will motivate your toddler to move out of nappies towards using a potty or toilet for themselves. Most children start to have awareness and muscle control in their second year. Signs they are ready include their nappy being dry for two hours, wanting more privacy when they are having a bowel movement (they may go off and hide when filling their nappy), and being able to tell you with words or gestures when they need changing.

1
Take a relaxed approach
Children have a drive to be independent. Trust that just as they wanted to learn to walk, they will master potty training too, and this will also take many steps. If you are anxious, your child will be too.

4
Role model it
When you feel the urge to go to the toilet, tell your toddler what it feels like in your body and where you feel it, so they start to recognize these signals too.

❝ ❞
CHILDREN START TO HAVE AWARENESS AND MUSCLE CONTROL IN THEIR SECOND YEAR.

WORKING THINGS OUT

8 key principles

2
Be open about it
To help your child feel comfortable, avoid using words like "yucky" or "dirty" about defecation. Studies show that speaking openly about wee and poo speeds the process up.

3
Help them be body aware
Point out where their bladder and bowels are and explain that wee and poo are kept here before they come out. Tell them that when they feel tingly or full in these places, it's a sign that it is time to go in the potty.

5
Look for cues
Watch out for your child pulling faces, tugging at their nappy, shuddering, squirming, squatting, shifting from foot to foot, or touching their genitals. When you spot these, ask if they feel it's time to go pee or poo, to help your toddler make the connection.

6
Make potty time fun
Make the shift from babyhood by now changing them in the bathroom only while they are standing up, as from now they will be upright when they use the potty or toilet. Point out how they are more comfortable without nappies so they make the connection.

7
Set the stage
Put a potty in the bathroom and explain it's a smaller version of the grown-ups' toilet. Say that poo is what's left over from our food and show them how you empty their dirty nappies into the bowl. Have toys or books about potty training only for use in the bathroom, and a fun hand-washing song for after.

8
Expect ups and downs
Young children are still developing muscle control. Accidents are part of the process. If they wet themselves, simply say, "Oops, your trousers are wet. I bet that feels cold." Or, "You noticed you needed the potty. You're doing a great job." Pause potty training if your child is resistant or getting upset; they may not be ready.

TAILORED ADVICE

Transition with pull-up nappies
Show them how to pull pants up and down by themselves. When they are ready, let them come with you to pick out their first underwear.

Think about diet
Give them plenty of fibre, including fruit and veg, and keep them hydrated, to make their stools softer and easier to pass.

Have a bottle of bubbles handy
Gently blowing bubbles can help children relax their pelvic floor muscles, which control urination and defecation.

Avoid a big fuss
Celebrating too much when your child uses the potty can feel pressurizing. Instead, warmly notice what they achieved with words like: "You listened to your body and you went to the potty to do a wee. You're learning really fast."

"WHY DOES MY TODDLER LOVE TO SING AND DANCE?"

Your baby has been tuned into the rhythm of music since before they were born. Now they are improving their coordination and balance, your toddler can start moving their body to a beat.

SCENARIO | When you put on a familiar song, you notice that your toddler dances and sings and wants you to join in.

Your baby was born with an innate ability to pick up a beat, and by 13 months, 90 per cent of parents have noticed their babies have enough coordination to move their bodies to music in a dancelike way.

Around 18 months, they are likely to add new moves, like shifting from side to side and twirling around. By now your toddler may start to sing in a more recognizable way, too. In their first year, they sang in response to you. By the age of one, they are singing higher and lower notes, though not yet in tune with the music. Through their second year, they will try to match the melody of the music.

WHAT YOU MIGHT BE THINKING

Why does my toddler sing along and dance when they hear music, even when we're out of the house? Are they musical or do all toddlers do this?

SEE RELATED TOPICS
Why does my baby like nursery rhymes?: pp.86-87

WHAT THEY MIGHT BE THINKING

● **When your toddler sings and dances**, it releases feel-good endorphins. As they do not yet feel self-consciousness, they will move freely and joyfully. Researchers have found that babies always smile as they dance.

● **Toddlers quickly realize that dancing is a social activity**, which their parents nearly always join in. This will help your toddler feel pleased and proud of themselves.

● **Your toddler now has more control over their voice**, thanks to the maturing of their vocal tract, and a bigger oral cavity, as well as more coordinated movements of their tongue and mouth muscles.

"Why does my toddler love to sing and dance?" 185

HOW YOU COULD RESPOND

In the moment

Play music with a clear beat
Research has found babies and toddlers respond more to the beat of music than the tune.

Dance along
Dancing with your child promotes closer attachment, according to studies. It boosts physical activity and agility and is an easy way to distract or entertain toddlers.

Use music to promote cooperation
Studies have found that children are more likely to help and cooperate after games that include synchronized movement. Try dancing together before challenging transitions in the day.

In the long term

Join a toddler dance class
Though your toddler will be delighted to dance at home, a class will help them learn more about spatial awareness and how to share space with others.

Find songs to extend vocabulary
Toddlers remember the words to songs long before they can speak in sentences. Sing songs with stories that will help extend their vocabulary and help them learn sequences.

> **" "**
> **THEY ARE LIKELY TO ADD NEW MOVES, LIKE SHIFTING FROM SIDE TO SIDE AND TWIRLING.**

"WHAT DO **NUMBERS** MEAN TO TODDLERS?"

We tend to believe that the sooner toddlers know their letters and numbers, the better. However, they won't yet understand what these symbols represent.

SCENARIO | You see your toddler putting three of their toy cars in a line. They seem to be counting them at the same time.

Your child was born with an innate ability to group together small numbers and see patterns. By now, your toddler is likely to have heard simple number sequences in songs, nursery rhymes, and books. So they are likely to be able to repeat the first five to ten numbers by rote, as well as repeat the first letters of the alphabet song, which they will also have heard.

However, it is too soon for them to cognitively understand the link between names of numbers and the quantities they represent – or letters and the sounds they make, and how they make up words. Aim to help your toddler become familiar with these symbols in lots of playful ways first, rather than try to push them into maths and reading before they are ready.

WHAT YOU MIGHT BE THINKING

My child already seems to be picking up their alphabet and numbers. Does this mean they're really clever?

"What do numbers mean to toddlers?" 187

WHAT THEY MIGHT BE THINKING

- **Your toddler has noticed you smile** and get excited when you hear them recite their numbers or say their alphabet, and so they may repeat them more to please you.

- **If you ask your toddler to hand them one toy**, it's likely they can do so. If you ask them to hand you three, they are not yet ready to count them out.

- **If your toddler feels you are trying to teach them something**, they will feel pressured, especially if you are asking them to do things they are not ready for.

- **If you show your toddler flashcards** with letters and numbers, they may start to recognize the shapes. But as letters are still an abstract concept, they won't yet understand what is represented.

SEE RELATED TOPICS
How fast is my toddler learning new words?: pp.188-189

HOW YOU COULD RESPOND

In the moment

Stick to small quantities
Accept they have learned their numbers by rote. It doesn't mean they can count. For now, counting out three objects is enough for them to start to grasp the concept of numbers.

Link numbers to the real world
Count out objects in different ways, whether it's the number of apples you put in the fruit bowl or the number of ducks in the bath. Sing number and letter songs, so they get their numbers and the alphabet in sequence more easily.

In the long term

Keep it simple with letters too
Stick to showing them the letters that make up their names, in different forms so that they get used to the overall shape of their name.

Avoid overwhelm
Rather than show them the whole alphabet now, put the letters of their name on the wall, or as magnets on the fridge. To get them used to shape of letters, look for a personalized name puzzle, so they feel the letters and learn to place them in their slots.

Help them learn how the highest number is the total
When counting you could say, "Do you see there are three dinosaurs? Three. Let's count them. One, two, three dinosaurs", stressing the three. Help them understand the highest number is the total, a key concept in learning to count.

Introduce size and quantity words
As they expand their vocabulary you can add in more words like "bigger" and "smaller" and "more" and "less".

Develop their "grouping"
Split small numbers into groups of objects, like dividing blocks into small groups of two or three, so they start to see the patterns of numbers by sight. Encourage your child to develop sorting skills by asking to sort similar objects into piles.

Resist rushing reading
Neuroscientists say the wiring necessary for reading often isn't in place until a child reaches between five and seven, so take it slowly. Concentrate on showing your child how much fun books can be – and encouraging them to interact with the pictures.

"HOW FAST IS MY TODDLER LEARNING NEW WORDS?"

After a long lead-up to your child saying their first words, it now seems like your toddler is learning a new word every day, even if they are still learning to say them clearly.

SCENARIO | Your toddler points at a banana, saying "nana". The next day, they say "bibi" while staring at the cupboard where your biscuits are kept.

Your child's rapid brain development is helping them go from understanding words to being able to say them too, and being able to pick them up far more quickly. The connections between the language centres in their brains are strengthening.

These regions are now able to talk to another faster because the connections between them are getting coated with myelin, a fatty substance that insulates them and allows messages to move more quickly. This means your toddler may only need to hear a new word a few times before they work out what it means. As they've started to crack the code of language, they are also working out how words go together and will say phrases like, "More juice".

WHAT YOU MIGHT BE THINKING

I wrote down every new word when my child started talking. Now they are saying so many new words that I can't track them anymore.

SEE RELATED TOPICS
Why does my toddler want the same book?: pp.144-145

WHAT THEY MIGHT BE THINKING

• **Your child has worked out that everything** has a name. They are excited that they can express their needs more easily now they can say more words.

• **Your toddler may use a new word** they are interested in, but quickly forget about it if they don't hear it again.

• **Towards their second birthday,** your toddler may feel so confident in their language abilities that they may become upset if they can't be understood.

• **If you keep correcting** or drawing attention to their mistakes, it could put your toddler off trying new words.

❝ ❞
YOUR TODDLER IS LEARNING BY TRIAL AND ERROR.

HOW YOU COULD RESPOND

In the moment

Chat to them
Use eye contact when you are together and connect with them as you narrate your day, pointing out the things that they are most drawn to.

Try to understand
As your toddler picks up new words, their pronunciation may be hard to understand. Tune in to the context and show you are trying to understand so they keep talking.

Recast, instead of correct
Your toddler is learning by trial and error. Say the words back using the correct pronunciation or grammar. For example, if your child says, "mo wa da", you could reply, "Would you like some more water?"

Use eye contact
Research shows they learn much more language when you address them directly, rather than watching screens.

In the long term

Play role play games together
This gives your toddler a wonderful opportunity to explore feelings and situations, as well as practise lots of new words. Play out experiences they have had – like going to a café or putting their toys to bed. Pause, listen, and give them time to respond so they don't feel rushed.

Be aware of your phone use
Studies have found that parents give just 25 per cent of their attention to their toddler when they are distracted by their phones. You will be much less likely to take part in "serve and return" conversations, which are so important at this age.

Avoid relying on screens
If they regularly watch screens instead of talking or playing, they are missing out on real-world experiences that would rapidly boost their language skills. If you do put them in front of a screen, choose content carefully.

PARENTS' SURVIVAL GUIDE

BILINGUAL BABIES

As infants are laying down the brain circuitry to be able to talk and understand words, they have an innate ability to absorb language.

Babies are born being able to tell the 800 sounds of every human language apart, although this ability starts to fade between six months and one year. So if you and your co-parent are fluent in more than one language, learning two – or even three – is likely to feel as natural to your infant as learning just one. This will bring your child a range of cognitive benefits even before they can talk, which will last throughout their lives.

Bilingual children have been found to have stronger communication skills and think more flexibly, because they experience different perspectives. They are also able to concentrate better as they get older and are up to a third faster at shifting attention and spotting visual changes. This is possibly because they have to watch caregivers' mouths to check which language they are speaking.

1
Make it a part of life
Babies need to hear a second, or less spoken, language continuously around 30 per cent of the time to become fully bilingual. One language will be more dominant.

4
Give them time
As much as possible, look at your child when you speak. When they can watch how your mouth moves to make the word, they can tell more easily which language you are speaking. If you ask a question, leave them plenty of time to answer.

> **MAKE SURE THE MAIN LANGUAGE YOU TALK TO YOUR BABY CONVEYS YOUR LOVE.**

WORKING THINGS OUT

8 key principles

2
Don't worry about mixing words
It's normal for your child to swap around languages or mix words, known as "code mixing". Young children will often fill in gaps by using the word most accessible to them in the moment.

3
Try one language/one parent
One way to make it simpler for you and your co-parent is for each parent to stick to one language each. If your child asks questions in one language, try answering in the one you normally use, to keep it consistent.

5
Try different languages in context
If you're the only parent who is bilingual, you could try using the second language at regular daily events like mealtimes, bath times, or nappy changes.

6
Teach them your mother tongue
Make sure that you are fluent enough in the main language you use with your baby to convey your warmth and love. These "feelings" words are essential for growing emotional intelligence.

7
Start as soon as possible
Your baby picked up the inflections of all the languages they heard in the womb. If you add another later, for example if you move to a new country, a toddler is still in the critical window for being able to learn a secondary language more easily.

8
Find new contexts
Take your child to visit native speakers in your family to show them it has a wider use beyond their relationship with you. The more ways your child hears all their languages used, the better.

TAILORED ADVICE

Play without pressuring
Avoid correcting your child if they use a wrong word. One language will always be behind the other, but if you keep correcting your child's mistakes, they may become reluctant to speak the one they know less well.

Avoid relying on tech
Though TV programmes and language apps may feel like an easy way to immerse them, children this age need to interact with real people to learn language.

Show the parallels
Offer books and sing songs and nursery rhymes in both languages, so they see the direct parallels. Play a game of missing out words for them to fill in.

"WHY IS MY TODDLER FASCINATED BY MY PHONE?"

As every parent knows, it's tempting to hand your toddler your phone to keep them quiet in stressful, busy moments. But it's wise to avoid giving them a screen as a toy at this critical stage of their development.

SCENARIO | On a long journey, your toddler screams they want to play on your phone in the back of the car.

Your toddler is going through enormous cognitive development, including how to talk, concentrate, and manage their emotions. At this age your child's brain learns best from face-to-face interactions.

The colourful pictures and activities on phones can seem much more gratifying, but think ahead. By handing your phone to your child as a plaything, they won't learn to entertain themselves. They will continue to expect screens as they get older and these expectations – and the conflicts they cause – are likely to scale up in size.

WHAT YOU MIGHT BE THINKING

This is stressful. I can't face a tantrum now. Is there any harm in just letting them go on my phone for a while?

WHAT THEY MIGHT BE THINKING

- **Your toddler may look skilful** as they move their fingers across the touch screen. However, the fast pace can make the real world feel boring by comparison.

- **Toddlers love their control over a phone** and will want the same mastery in real life, leading them to become frustrated more quickly when reality doesn't feel the same.

- **If your toddler sees you on your phone a lot**, and observes you being mesmerized and entertained by it, they are more likely to want to copy you.

- **A child watching an object**, like a ball, move across the screen, is only seeing it in two dimensions. They are not learning about how it moves through space, how it slows down, or how to grasp and manipulate it, as they would in the real world.

HOW YOU COULD RESPOND

In the moment

Keep real life more interesting
If you hand your phone to your child, you will be sending them the message that you give in if they make enough fuss. Instead, let them know how much there is to see and do on the journey. Ask them to look out of the window. Tell them what you see. Put on a song for a singalong. Even though it feels harder, it will teach your child the real-world – and connecting with you – is more fun.

Manage your expectations
Travelling with toddlers is always going to be challenging because they are restrained for long periods and feel powerless. Think of ways to break up the journey, or drive when they are due to sleep.

In the long term

Keep an eye on behaviour changes
Notice if your child is more bad-tempered, shows less interest in toys, or has trouble sleeping after using screens – a reminder that phones are a short-term fix.

Make your phone boring
There are lots of ways to make phones less attractive to your toddler, like changing to monochrome and limiting apps to must-haves. Make your phone a tool, not a toy. Keep it out of sight, or on silent, when with your child as much as you can.

Avoid using it as your entertainment
If you often disappear into your phone, your child will feel rejected and miss out on hours of face-to-face contact, connection, and language learning.

Delay screen use
Some research has found that learning apps may help children recognize letters sooner – but at this age, letters and numbers are an abstract concept. Other studies found that children this age who regularly use screens have smaller vocabularies.

SEE RELATED TOPICS
Screen time: pp.196-197

> " "
> **THE COLOURFUL ACTIVITIES ON PHONES CAN SEEM GRATIFYING, BUT THINK AHEAD.**

"WHY DOES MY TODDLER HAVE SO MUCH ENERGY?"

Now your toddler has mastered balance and walking, they are keen to use their newfound abilities to practise running, jumping, and climbing too.

SCENARIO | Your toddler is running around, shouting, and finding things to jump and climb on. You're finding it hard to keep up.

Adjusted for body mass, toddlers burn the most calories a day for their size than at any other stage of development. Your toddler now has more energy than possibly any other time of life. They are also driven to move a lot to build their muscles.

On top of that, they are still developing the frontal lobes, which helps put the brakes on physical behaviour. So even if you ask them to slow down, they will find it hard to control their impulse to move. Rather than be annoyed by your child's energy, offer outlets for it. If you join them from time to time, you can create some memorable moments during this most active phase.

WHAT YOU MIGHT BE THINKING

My toddler never seems to stop. It's exhausting because I have to constantly watch them in case they hurt themselves.

SEE RELATED TOPICS
Why does my toddler love to take risks?: pp.146-147

WHAT THEY MIGHT BE THINKING

◉ **Your toddler has learned to run and jump** and now wants to test what they can do.

◉ **By around two**, your toddler can run more quickly and change direction. So they are excited to be chased by you.

◉ **Your child is practising "maximum effort"**, a drive to push themselves to their physical limits to develop key skills. They may try carrying things that are too heavy for them, or climb play equipment before they are ready.

◉ **Running around is a key** way for your toddler to let out emotions. However, when they get tired, this will trigger their cortisol levels, making them even more excitable.

HOW YOU COULD RESPOND

In the moment

Meet them where they are
Offer your child the space they need to run around in bursts throughout the day. Once they've exhausted themselves, be the secure base they can return to.

Get them outside
Toddlers will use more energy outside, and use more of the seeking part of their brain, making it more tiring. Studies show that children are more cooperative outside, and sleep better afterwards.

Create play opportunities inside too
Create a safe soft play space with floor cushions, bean bags, or soft balls, so you can relax about them being active.

Have realistic expectations
For this period, consider putting off taking them to weddings or other adult-centred events until they can regulate themselves in keeping with their environment.

In the long term

Share the care
Research has found dads tend to play in more physical ways than mums. Rough and tumble games are a key way for toddlers to practise their strength and learn physical self-control.

Frame it positively
Celebrate your child's energy as a positive sign of how much they enjoy using their bodies. Avoid generalizations about sons being more boisterous than daughters.

Offer a balanced diet
Think about how to keep your child's blood sugar levels constant by offering lots of fibre-rich whole foods, which are more slow release. Keep sweets a treat.

Help your child regulate
Have a routine at the end of the day to help them settle, whether that's with gentle songs or quiet story time.

> **CELEBRATE YOUR CHILD'S ENERGY.**

PARENTS' SURVIVAL GUIDE

SCREEN TIME

Screen technology can offer your child countless ways to learn and find out information. But at this critical stage of their development, it's important they learn how the world works through real interactions with you.

They also need to use their bodies and their five senses to explore the physical environment and find out how to move within it. Furthermore, your child is also still developing the ability to choose what to pay attention to and how to concentrate. Research has found the bright animations found on phones and tablets, which move fast and provide constant stimuli, interrupt this process. For now, delay giving your child screens as entertainment. This is a precious period of discovering the real world through experiencing it, not from a digital device.

1
Screen time is a health issue
Think about what inputs you want to feed your child's brain – and whether you want them to learn in the real world or from tech created for profit.

4
Think about the effect on sleep
One study with six- to 36-month-old children found that as the amount of time spent using touch screens increased, the longer it took them to get to sleep and the less they slept.

> " "
> YOUR CHILD'S BEST LEARNING TOOL WILL ALWAYS BE YOU.

WORKING THINGS OUT
8 key principles

2
Make real life more fun
Children learn best in person. Their optimum learning tool will always be you. Offer lots of face-to-face contact and conversation. This is not only how your child learns to talk. It develops essential social skills.

3
Give your child time to develop concentration
Children need to focus in the moment so they can learn to concentrate. This is the foundation for all learning and problem solving. Giving toddlers screens interrupts this development, according to research.

5
Delay screens
The longer you delay giving screens as a source of entertainment, the sooner your child will be able to talk and the more words they will know.

6
Make video calls the exception
As early as six months, babies can tell when a person on a screen is interacting directly with them – so this exception may benefit your child. If you have friends or relatives who live far away, keep in touch with two-way conversations on screen.

7
Make careful choices
There may be times when you need a break. Be selective about what entertainment you set up for your child. Aim for a time-limited amount of slow-paced, high-quality educational television designed specifically for their age group.

8
Take the longer view
While a phone may seem like a quick fix to calm your screaming toddler in a confined space, keep an eye on the bigger picture. In the long run, your parenting will be easier if you set clear boundaries now, rather than try to rein back their usage when they are older.

TAILORED ADVICE

Limit your own screen use in front of your child
Use phones and tablets as little as practically possible. Your child will feel rejected if you find screens more interesting than them.

Avoid having screens on in the background
If you have a screen on in your home, you will talk less to your child. You will also be less likely to notice cues that they are hungry, tired, or lonely, resulting in more meltdowns.

Be there with them
If you want to introduce some screen entertainment, try and sit with them, and talk about what they are seeing.

Help them fall in love with books
Join the library to help your child fall in love with books and learn to discover new interests through the printed page too.

BIBLIOGRAPHY

Introduction

Bakermans-Kranenburg MJ, Lotz A, Alyousefi-van Dijk K, van IJzendoorn M. (2019). Birth of a Father: Fathering in the First 1,000 Days. Child Dev Perspect. 13(4):247-253.

Bowlby, J. (1988). A Secure Base: Parent-Child Attachment and Healthy Human Development, New York, Basic Books

Dekaban, A.S. and Sadowsky, D. (1978). Changes in brain weights during the span of human life: relation of brain weights to body heights and body weights, Ann. By the age of two, a child's brain is about 70 to 80 per cent of its adult size. Neurology, 4:345-356.

Hoff, E (2005). Language Experience and Language Milestones During Early Childhood. In K. McCartney & D. Phillips (Eds). Two to three year olds may be learning as many as eight to ten new words a day: Blackwell Handbook of early childhood development: Blackwell Publishing.

Chapter 1: Your 0–6-month-old

Cavallini A, Fazzi E, Viviani V, Astori MG, Zaverio S, Bianchi PE, Lanzi G. (2002). Visual acuity in the first two years of life in healthy term newborns: an experience with the teller acuity cards. Funct Neurol. 17(2):87-92

Del Giudice, Marco (2011). Alone in the dark? Modeling the conditions for visual experience in human fetuses. Developmental psychobiology 53.2 :214-219

Johnson SP. (2010). How Infants Learn About the Visual World. Cogn Sci. 34(7): 1158-1184

Graven (2008): Visual Development in the Human Fetus, Infant, and Young Child

Glass, P. (2002). Development of the visual system and implications for intervention. Infants and Young Children, 15, 1–10

Morgan, J. (2017). Womb with a view: Sensory development in utero | Your Pregnancy Matters | UT Southwestern Medical Center. utswmed.org.

Reid, Vincent M., et al. (2017). The human fetus preferentially engages with face-like visual stimuli. Current Biology 27.12: 1825 1828

Held R, Birch E, Gwiazda J. (1980). Stereoacuity of human infants. Proc Natl Acad Sci U S A. 77(9):5572-4

Lasky, R.E. and Williams, A.L. (2005). The Development of the Auditory System from Conception to Term. NeoReviews, 6(3), pp.e141–e152

Nagy E, Thompson P, Mayor L, and Doughty H. (2021). Do foetuses communicate? Foetal responses to interactive versus non-interactive maternal voice and touch: An exploratory analysis. Infant Behav Dev. 63:101562

Neshat H, Jebreili M, Seyyedrasouli A, Ghojazade M, Hosseini MB, Hamishehkar H. (2016). Effects of Breast Milk and Vanilla Odors on Premature Neonate's Heart Rate and Blood Oxygen Saturation During and After Venipuncture. Pediatr Neonatol. 57(3):225-31

Nishitani S, Miyamura T, Tagawa M, Sumi M, Takase R, Doi H, Moriuchi H, and Shinohara K. (2009). The calming effect of a maternal breast milk odor on the human newborn infant. Neurosci Res. 63(1):66-71

Chen, C.-Y., Harrison, T., McNally, M. and Heathcock, J.C. (2021). Preliminary evidence of voicean association between spontaneous kicking and learning in infants between 3–4 months of age. Brazilian Journal of Physical Therapy, 25(3), pp.329–335

Thomason, M.E., Hect, J., Waller, R., Manning, J.H., Stacks, A.M., Beeghly, M., Boeve, J.L., Wong, K., van den Heuvel, M.I., Hernandez-Andrade, E., Hassan, S.S. and Romero, R. (2018). Prenatal neural origins of infant motor development: Associations between fetal brain and infant motor development. Development and Psychopathology, 30(3), pp.763–772

Van der Meer, a L. (1997). Keeping the arm in the limelight: advanced visual control of arm movements in neonates. European Journal of Paediatric Neurology : EJPN : Official Journal of the European Paediatric Neurology Society, 1(4), 103–8

Von Hofsten C. (1989). Mastering reaching and grasping: The development of manual skills in infancy. InAdvances in psychology (Vol. 61, pp. 223-258). North-Holland

Als, H., Duffy, F.H., McAnulty, G.B., Rivkin, M.J., Vajapeyam, S., Mulkern, R.V., Warfield, S.K., Huppi, P.S., Butler, S.C., Conneman, N., Fischer, C., & Eichenwald, E.C. (2004). Early experience alters brain function and structure. Pediatrics, 113(4), 846-857

Aslam M et al. (2007). Development of Fetal Senses: Implication in Intrauterine and Postnatal Life. Neonatal Intensive Care: Journal of Perinatology-neonatology. 20 (4): 18-20

Marx V et al. (2015). Fetal Behavioural Responses to Maternal Voice and Touch. PLoS One. 10 (6)

Vittner, D et al. (2019). Parent Engagement Correlates with Parent and Preterm Infant Oxytocin Release during Skin-to-Skin Contact. Advances in Neonatal Care. 19 (1): 73–79

Scatliffe N et al. (2019). Oxytocin and early parent-infant interactions: A systematic review. International Journal of Nursing Sciences. 6 (4):445-453

Brummelte, S., Chau, C.M.Y., Cepeda, I.L., Degenhardt, A., Weinberg, J., Synnes, A.R., & Grunau, R.E. (2015). Cortisol levels in former preterm children are predicted by neonatal procedural pain-related stress. Psychoneuroendocrinology, 51, 151-163.

Conde-Agudelo A, Díaz-Rossello JL. (2016). Kangaroo mother care to reduce morbidity and mortality in low birthweight infants. Cochrane Database of Systematic Reviews 2016, Issue 8. Art. No.: CD002771.

Döra Ö, Büyük ET. (2021). Effect of White Noise and Lullabies on Pain and Vital Signs in Invasive Interventions Applied to Premature Babies. Pain Manag Nurs ;22:724-9

Feijo L et al. (2006). Mothers' depressed mood and anxiety levels are reduced after massaging their preterm infants. Infant Behavior and Development. 29:476-480

Field T. (2012). Infant Massage. Touch. Cambridge, Mass.: MIT, 2014. 152-153. Print; Ang, JY., et al. A randomized placebo-controlled trial of massage therapy on the immune system of preterm infants. Pediatrics130:e1549-e1558

McMahon E, Wintermark P, Lahav A. (2012). Auditory brain development in premature infants: the importance of early experience. Ann N Y Acad Sci. 1252:17-24.

Williamson S, McGrath JM. (2019). What Are the Effects of the Maternal Voice on Preterm Infants in the NICU? Adv Neonatal Care. 19:294-310.

Diego M., Field T, Hernandez-Reif. M. (2010). Preterm Infant Massage Therapy Research: A Review. Infant Behav Dev. 33(2): 115–124

Liao J, Liu G, Xie N, et al. (2021). Mothers' voices and white noise on premature infants' physiological reactions in a neonatal intensive care unit: A multi-arm randomized controlled trial. Int J Nurs Stud. 119:103934

Milgrom, J., Newnham, C., Anderson, P.J., Doyle, L.W., Gemmill, A.W., Lee, K., Hunt, R.W., Bear, M., & Inder, T. (2010). Early sensitivity training for parents of preterm infants: Impact on the developing brain. Pediatric Research, 67(3), 330-335

Wachman, E.M. and Lahav, A. (2010). The effects of noise on preterm infants in the NICU. Archives of Disease in Childhood - Fetal and Neonatal Edition, 96(4), pp.F305–F309

White-Traut RC, Nelson MN, Silvestri JM, et al. (2002). Effect of auditory, tactile, visual, and vestibular intervention on length of stay, alertness, and feeding progression in preterm infants. Dev Med Child Neurol. 44:91-97

Futagi, Y., Toribe, Y. and Suzuki, Y. (2012). The Grasp Reflex and Moro Reflex in Infants: Hierarchy of Primitive Reflex Responses. International Journal of Pediatrics, 2012, pp.1–10.

Glodowski KR, Thompson RH, Martel L. (2019). The rooting reflex as an infant feeding cue. J Appl Behav Anal. 52(1):17-27

Geddes, D. T., & Sakalidis, V. S. (2015). Breastfeeding: how do they do it? Infant sucking, swallowing and breathing. Infant Journal, 11(5), 146- 150

DeCasper, A. and Fifer, W. (1980). Of human bonding: newborns prefer their mothers' voices. Science, 208(4448), pp.1174–1176

Erickson, L.C. and Newman, R.S. (2017). Influences of Background Noise on Infants and Children. Current Directions in Psychological Science, 26(5), pp.451–457

Graham AM, Fisher PA, Pfeifer JH. (2013). What sleeping babies hear: a functional MRI study of interparental conflict and infants' emotion processing

Graven, S.N. and Browne, J.V. (2008). Auditory Development in the Fetus and Infant. Newborn and Infant Nursing Reviews, 8(4), pp.187–193.

Grossmann T. (2010). The development of emotion perception in face and voice during infancy. Restor Neurol Neurosci. 28(2):219-3

Nagy E, Thompson P, Mayor L, and Doughty H. (2021). Do foetuses communicate? Foetal responses to interactive versus non-interactive maternal voice and touch: An exploratory analysis. Infant Behav Dev. 63:101562

Querleu, D., Lefebvre, C., Titran, M., Renard, X., Morillion, M., and Crepin, G. (1984). Reaction of the newborn infant less than 2 hours after birth to the maternal voice. J. Gynecol. Obstet. Biol. Reprod. (Paris) 13, 125–134

Rao, W.-W., Zhu, X.-M., Zong, Q.-Q., Zhang, Q., Hall, B.J., Ungvari, G.S. and Xiang, Y.-T. (2020). Prevalence of prenatal and postpartum depression in fathers: A comprehensive meta-analysis of observational surveys. Journal of Affective Disorders, 263, pp.491–499.

Bruderer, A.G., Danielson, D.K., Kandhadai, P. and Werker, J.F. (2015). Sensorimotor influences on speech perception in infancy. Proceedings of the National Academy of Sciences, 112(44), pp.13531–13536.

Barker, L. (2023). New survey shows 9 in 10 parents co-sleep but less than half know how to reduce the risk of SIDS. The Lullaby Trust.

Bartick, M., Young, M., Louis-Jacques, A., McKenna, J.J. and Ball, H.L. (2022). Bedsharing may partially explain the reduced risk of sleep-related death in breastfed infants. Frontiers in Pediatrics,

Blair, PS, Sidebotham, P, Pease, A & Fleming, P. (2014). Bed-Sharing in the Absence of Hazardous Circumstances: Is There a Risk of Sudden Infant Death Syndrome? An Analysis from Two Case-Control Studies Conducted in the UK. PLOS One.

McKenna et al. (2001). Mother-Infant Cosleeping: Toward a New Scientific Beginning, by James J. McKenna and Sarah Mosko. Ch. 16 in Sudden Infant Death Syndrome: Puzzles, Problems and Possibilities. R. Byard and H. Krous, eds. London: Arnqld Publishers

Morgan, B.E., Horn, A.R. and Bergman, N.J. (2011). Should Neonates Sleep Alone? Biological Psychiatry, 70(9), pp.817–825.

Vennemann, MM, Bajanowski, T, Brinkmann, B, Jorch, G, Yücesan, K, Sauerland, C, & Mitchell, EA. (2009). Does breastfeeding reduce the risk of sudden infant death syndrome? Pediatrics, 123(3), e406–10.

Barrera, M.E. and Maurer, D. (1981). Recognition of Mother's Photographed Face by the Three-Month-Old Infant. Child Development, 52(2), p.714.

Carnevali, L., Gui, A., Jones, E.J.H. and Farroni, T. (2022). Face Processing in Early Development: A Systematic Review of Behavioral Studies and Considerations in Times of COVID-19 Pandemic. Frontiers in Psychology, 13.

Field T. M., et al. (1984). Mother-stranger face discrimination by the newborn. Infant Behavior and Development, 7, 19-25

Mills M., & Melhuish E. (1974). Recognition of mother's voice in early infancy. Nature, 252, 123-124

Heck, A., Chroust, A., White, H., Jubran, R. and Bhatt, R.S. (2018). Development of body emotion perception in infancy: From discrimination to recognition. Infant Behavior and Development, 50, pp.42–51.

Pascalis, O., Scott, L.S., Kelly, D.J., Shannon, R.W., Nicholson, E., Coleman, M. and Nelson, C.A. (2005). Plasticity of face processing in infancy. Proceedings of the National Academy of Sciences, 102(14), pp.5297–5300.

Spencer, J.A., Moran, D.J., Lee, A. and Talbert, D. (1990). White noise and sleep induction. Archives of Disease in Childhood, 65(1), pp.135–137.

Young, K.S., Parsons, C.E., Jegindoe Elmholdt, E.-M., Woolrich, M.W., van Hartevelt, T.J., Stevner, A.B.A., Stein, A. and Kringelbach, M.L. (2015). Evidence for a Caregiving Instinct: Rapid Differentiation of Infant from Adult Vocalizations Using Magnetoencephalography. Cerebral Cortex, 26(3), pp.1309–1321.

Ana Laguna, Sandra Pusil, Àngel Bazán, Jonathan Adrián Zegarra-Valdivia, Anna Lucia Paltrinieri, Paolo Piras, Clàudia Palomares i Perera, Alexandra Pardos Véglia, Oscar Garcia-Algar, Silvia Orlandi (2023). Multi-modal analysis of infant cry types characterization: Acoustics, body language and brain signals, Computers in Biology and Medicine, Volume 167, 107626, ISSN 0010-4825.

Lee, S., Matsumori, K., Nishimura, K., Nishimura, Y., Ikeda, Y., Eto, T. and Higuchi, S. (2018). Melatonin suppression and sleepiness in children exposed to blue-enriched white LED lighting at night. Physiological Reports, 6(24), p.e13942.

So K, Adamson TM, Horne RS. (2007). The use of actigraphy for the assessment of the development of sleep/wake patterns in infants during the first 12 months of life. Journal of Sleep Research. 16:181–187.

Thomas, K.A., Burr, R.L., Spieker, S., Lee, J. and Chen, J. (2014). Mother–infant circadian rhythm: Development of individual patterns and dyadic synchrony. Early Human Development, 90(12), pp.885–890.

Pennestri, M. H., Laganière, C., Bouvette-Turcot, A. A., Pokhvisneva, I., Steiner, M., Meaney, M. J., Gaudreau, H., & Mavan Research Team (2018). Uninterrupted Infant Sleep, Development, and Maternal Mood. Pediatrics, 142(6), e20174330

Wong, S.D., Wright, K.P., Spencer, R.L., Vetter, C., Hicks, L.M., Jenni, O.G. and LeBourgeois, M.K. (2022). Development of the circadian system in early life: maternal and environmental factors. Journal of Physiological Anthropology, 41(1).

Gerhardt, S. (2004). Why Love Matters, How Affection Shapes a Baby's Brain, Routledge

Gunnar, M.R. and Donzella, B. (2002). Social regulation of the cortisol levels in early human development. Psychoneuroendocrinology, 27(1-2), pp.199–220.

Mednick S., PhD. (2017). Author of Take a Nap! Change Your Life; assistant professor of psychiatry, University of California, San Diego

Naska, A., et al. (2007). Siestas of Health Adults and Coronary Mortality in the General Population. Archives of Internal Medicine

Panksepp, J. (1998). Affective neuroscience. New York: Oxford University Press

Schore, A.N. (2001). The effects of early relational trauma on right brain development, affect regulation, and infant mental health. Infant Mental Health Journal, 22, 201-269

Sunderland, M. (2006). The Science of Parenting, DK Books

Zhang, S. and He, C. (2023). Effect of the sound of the mother's heartbeat combined with white noise on heart rate, weight, and sleep in premature infants: a retrospective comparative cohort study. Annals of Palliative Medicine, 12(1), pp.11120–11120.

Clavadetscher JE, Brown AM, Ankrum C, Teller DY. (1988). Spectral sensitivity and chromatic discriminations in 3- and 7-week-old human infants. J Opt Soc Am A. 5(12):2093-105

Di Giorgio E, Lunghi M, Vallortigara G, and Simion F. (2021). Newborns' sensitivity to speed changes as a building block for animacy perception. Sci Rep. 11(1):542

Farroni T, Csibra G, Simion F, et al. (2002). Eye contact detection in humans from birth. Proc Natl Acad Sci U S A. 99 14:9602-9605

Bristow, D., Dehaene-Lambertz, G., Mattout, J., Soares, C., Gliga, T., Baillet, S. and Mangin, J.-F. (2008). Hearing Faces: How the Infant Brain Matches the Face It Sees with the Speech It Hears. Journal of Cognitive Neuroscience, 21(5), pp.905–921.

Jandó G, Mikó-Baráth E, Markó K, Hollódy K, Török B, Kovacs I. (2012). Early-onset binocularity in preterm infants reveals experience-dependent visual development in humans. Proc Natl Acad Sci USA. 109(27):11049-52

Moore, E. R., Bergman, N., Anderson, G. C., & Medley, N. (2016). Early skin-to-skin contact for mothers and their healthy newborn infants. Cochrane Database of Systematic Reviews.

Ferjan R, N., Lytle, S.R. and Kuhl, P.K. (2020). Parent coaching increases conversational turns and advances infant language development. Proceedings of the National Academy of Sciences, 117(7), pp.3484–3491.

Tamis-LeMonda, C.S., Kuchirko, Y. and Song, L. (2014). Why Is Infant Language Learning Facilitated by Parental Responsiveness? Current Directions in Psychological Science, 23(2), pp.121–126.

Pelaez, M. and Monlux, K. (2018). Development of Communication in Infants: Implications for Stimulus Relations Research. Perspectives on Behavior Science,41(1), pp.175–188.

Heimann M., Nelson K. E., Schaller J. (1989). Neonatal imitation of tongue protrusion and mouth opening: methodological aspects and evidence of early individual differences. Scand. J. Psychol. 30, 90–101.

Hess U., Blairy S. (2001). Facial mimicry and emotional contagion to dynamic emotional facial expressions and their influence on decoding accuracy. Int. J. Psychophysiol. 40, 129–141.

Horne P. J., Erjavec M. (2007). Do infants show generalized imitation of gestures? J. Exp. Anal. Behav. 87, 63–87.

Kawakami, F. and Yanaihara, T. (2012). Smiles in the fetal period. Infant Behavior and Development, 35(3), pp.466–471.

Nagy, E., Pilling, K., Blake, V. and Orvos, H. (2019). Positive evidence for neonatal imitation: A general response, adaptive engagement. Developmental Science, 23(2)

Steiner, J. E. (1974). Discussion paper: Innate, discriminative human facial expressions to taste and smell stimulation. Annals of the New York Academy of Sciences, 237, 229–233.

Illingworth, R.S. and Lutz, W. (1965). Head circumference of infants related to body weight. Archives of Disease in Childhood, 40(214), pp.672–676.

Siegel, D.N., Ogle, M.M., Wilson, C., Scholes, O., Prow, A. and Mannen, E.M. (2024). How do babies roll? Identifying the coordinated movements of infant rolling through video compared to laboratory techniques. Technology and Health Care, 32(4), pp.2527–2539.

Cullen, C, Field, T, Escalona, A & Hartshorn, K. (2000). Father-infant interactions are enhanced by massage therapy. Early Child Development and Care, Vol 164, 2000. pp. 41-47

Cheng C.D., Volk A.A., Marini Z.A. (2011). Supporting Fathering through Infant Massage. J. Perinat. Educ. 20:200–209.

Conde-Agudelo A. and Díaz-Rossello JL. (2016). Kangaroo mother care to reduce morbidity and mortality in low birthweight infants. Cochrane Database Syst Rev. 23;(8):CD002771

Feldman R, Singer M, and Zagoory O. (2010). Touch attenuates infants' physiological reactivity to stress. Dev Sci. 13(2):271-8

Field, T. (2002). Infants' Need for Touch. Human Development, 45(2), pp.100–103. .

Gürol A., Polat S. (2012). The Effects of Baby Massage on Attachment between Mother and Their Infants. Asian Nurs. Res. 6:35–41.

Holditch-Davis D., White-Traut R.C., Levy J.A., O'Shea T.M., Geraldo V., David R.J. (2014). Maternally Administered Interventions for Preterm Infants in the Nicu: Effects on Maternal Psychological Distress and Mother–Infant Relationship. Infant Behav. Dev. 37:695–710.

Jönsson EH, Kotilahti K, Heiskala J, Wasling HB, Olausson H, Croy I, Mustaniemi H, Hiltunen P, Tuulari JJ, Scheinin NM, Karlsson L, Karlsson H, Nissilä I. (2018). Affective and non-affective touch evoke differential brain responses in 2-month-old infants. Neuroimage. 169:162-171

Johnston C, Campbell-Yeo M, Disher T, Benoit B, Fernandes A, Streiner D, Inglis D, Zee R. (2017). Skin-to-skin care for procedural pain in neonates. Cochrane Database Syst Rev. 2:CD008435

Lestari, K.P., Nurbadlina, F.R., Wagiyo, W. and Jauhar, M. (2021). The effectiveness of baby massage in increasing infant's body weight. Journal of Public Health Research, 10(s1).

Nahidi F., Gazerani N., Yousefi P., Abadi A.R. (2017). The Comparison of the Effects of Massaging and Rocking on Infantile Colic. Iran. J. Nurs. Midwifery Res. 22:67.

Packheiser, J., Hartmann, H., Fredriksen, K., Gazzola, V., Keysers, C. and Michon, F. (2024). A systematic review and multivariate meta-analysis of the physical and mental health benefits of touch interventions. Nature Human Behaviour, 8, pp.1–20.

Pickles A, Sharp H, Hellier J, Hill J. (2017). Prenatal anxiety, maternal stroking in infancy, and symptoms of emotional and behavioral disorders at 3.5 years. Eur Child Adolesc Psychiatry. 26(3):325-334

Romantshik O, Porter RH, Tillmann V, Varendi H. (2007). Preliminary evidence of a sensitive period for olfactory learning by human newborns. Acta Pædiatrica. 96(3):372 – 376

Sann C and Streri A. (2008). The limits of newborn's grasping to detect texture in a cross-modal transfer task. Infant Behav Dev. 31(3):523-31

Chapter 2: Your 6–12-month-old

Belsky J, Most RJ. (1981). From exploration to play: A cross-sectional study of infant free play behavior. Developmental Psychology. 17:630–639.

Fagan, M.K. and Iverson, J.M. (2007). The Influence of Mouthing on Infant Vocalization. Infancy : the official journal of the International Society on Infant Studies, 11(2), pp.191–202.

Fessler, D.M.T. and Abrams, E.T. (2004). Infant mouthing behavior: the immunocalibration hypothesis. Medical Hypotheses, 63(6), pp.925–932.

Klis, Anika van der, Adriaans Frans , Kager René (2023). Infants' behaviours elicit different verbal, nonverbal, and multimodal responses from caregivers during early play,Infant Behavior and Development, Volume 71, 101828, ISSN 0163-6383,

Goldfield, E.C. (2000). Exploration of vocal tract properties during serial production of vowels by full term and preterm infants. Infant Behavior and Development, 23(3-4), pp.421–439.

Kuhl, P.K. and Meltzoff, A.N. (1996). Infant vocalizations in response to speech: Vocal imitation and developmental change. The Journal of the Acoustical Society of America, 100(4 0 1), pp.2425–2438. Available at:

Laing, C. and Bergelson, E. (2020). From babble to words: Infants' early productions match words and objects in their environment. Cognitive Psychology, 122, p.101308.

Lieberman P, Crelin ES, Klatt DH (1972). Phonetic ability and related anatomy of the newborn and adult human. Neanderthal man, and the chimpanzee. Am Anthropol. 74:287–307.

Mugitani, R. and Hiroya, S. (2012). Development of vocal tract and acoustic features in children. Acoustical Science and Technology, 33(4), pp.215–220.

Prakash, M. and Johnny, Jc. (2015). Whats special in a child's larynx? Journal of Pharmacy and Bioallied Sciences, 7(5), p.55.

Sasaki CT, Levine PA, Laitman JT, Crelin ES. (1977). Postnatal descent of the epiglottis in man. Arch Otolaryngol. 103:169–171

H. Sigmundsson, B. Hopkins (2010). Baby swimming: exploring the effects of early intervention on subsequent motor abilities. Child: Care, Health and Development. 36 (3): 428

Baby Sleep Advice. (n.d.). Sonia Rochel of Thalasso Baby Bath shares her Bathing Techniques. https://www.baby-sleep-advice.com/sonia-rochel-thalasso-baby-bath.html

Blume-Peytavi U, Cork M, Faergemann J, et al. (2009). Bathing and cleansing newborns from day 1 to first year of life: recommendations from a European round table meeting. J Eur Acad Dermatol

Blossfeld I, Collins A, Kiely M, Delahunty C. (2007). Texture preferences of 12-month-old infants and role of early experiences. Food Qual Pref. 18:396–404. 10.1016/j.foodqual.2006.03.022

Borowitz, S.M. (2021). First Bites—Why, When, and What Solid Foods to Feed Infants. Frontiers in Pediatrics, 9(654171).

Field, L.B., Carraway, T., Hart, K., Malphurs, S., Rosenstein, J., Pelaez-Nogueras,M., Coletta, M., Ott, F., Hernandez-Reif, D. (1998). Food texture preferences in infants versus toddlers. Early Child Development and Care, Vol 146, pp. 69-85

Howard, A.J., Mallan, K.M., Byrne, R., Magarey A. & Daniels, L.A. (2012). Toddlers' food preferences. The impact of novel food exposure, maternal preferences and food neophobia. Appetite, Vol 59(3), Dec, 2012. pp. 818-825

Lundy, B., Field, T., Carraway, K., Hart, S., Malphurs, J., Rosenstein, M., Pelaez-Nogueras, M., Coletta, F., Ott, D. and Hernandez-Reif, M. (1998). Food Texture Preferences in Infants Versus Toddlers. Early Child Development and Care, 146(1), pp.69–85.

Mura Paroche, M., Caton, S.J., Vereijken, C.M.J.L., Weenen, H. and Houston-Price, C. (2017). How Infants and Young Children Learn About Food: A Systematic Review. Frontiers in Psychology, 8(1046).

Skinner, J.C., Carruth, B.R., Moran, J., Houck, K., Schmidhammer, J., Reed, A., Coletta, F., Cotter, R. & Ott, D. (1998). Toddlers' food preferences: Concordance with family members' preferences. Journal of Nutrition Education, Vol 30(1), pp. 17-22

Wright, C.M., Parkinson, K.N., Shipton, K.N. &Drewett, R.B. (2007). How do toddler eating problems relate to their eating behavior, food preferences, and growth? Pediatrics, Vol 120(4), pp. E1069-e1075

Adolph K, Vereijken B, Denny MA. (1998). Learning to crawl. Child Dev. 69(5):1299-312

Kretch, K.S., Franchak, J.M. and Adolph, K.E. (2013). Crawling and Walking Infants See the World Differently. Child Development, 85(4), pp.1503–1518.

Robson P. (1984). Pre-walking locomotor movements and their use in predicting standing and walking. Child Care Health Dev. 198410(5):317-30

Størvold GV, Aarethun K, Bratberg GH. (2013). Age for onset of walking and prewalking strategies. Early Hum Dev. 89(9):655-9.

Gopnik A. (2001): How Babies Think: The Science of Childhood:

Kuhl, P.K. (2015). How Babies Learn Language. Scientific American.

Reilly, S., Eadie, P., Bavin, E.L., Wake, M., Prior, M., Williams, J., Bretherton, L., Barrett, Y., & Ukoumunne, O.C. (2006). Growth of infant communication between 8 and 12 months: A population study. Journal of Paediatrics and Child Health, 42, 764-770.

Amsterdam, B. (1972). Mirror self-image reactions before age two. Developmental Psychobiology, 5(4), pp.297–305.

Bahrick, L. E., & Moss, L. (1996). Development of visual self-recognition in infancy. Ecological Psychology, 8(3), 189-208

Chinn, L.K., Noonan, C.F., Patton, K.S. and Lockman, J.J (2024). Tactile localization promotes infant self-recognition in the mirror-mark test. Current Biology, 34(6), pp.1370-1375.e2.

Chinn, L.K., Noonan, C.F. and Lockman, J.J. (2020). The Human Face Becomes Mapped as a Sensorimotor Reaching Space During the First Year. Child Development, 92(2), pp.760–773.

Priel, B., & de Schonen, S. (1986). Self-recognition: A study of a population without mirrors. Journal of experimental child psychology, 41(2), 237-250

Rigato, S., De Sepulveda, R., Richardson, E. and Maria Laura Filippetti (2024). This is me! Neural correlates of self-recognition in 6- to 8-month-old infants. Child development.

Schulman, A. H., Kaplowitz, C. (1977). Mirror-image response during the first two years of life. Developmental Psychobiology, 10(3), 133-142

Cirelli L.K., Trehub S.E. (2020). Familiar songs reduce infant distress. Dev. Psychol. 56(5):861–868.

De l'Etoile S.K. (2006). Infant-directed singing: a theory for clinical intervention. Music Ther. Perspect. 24(1):22–29.

Fancourt, D. and Perkins, R. (2018). The effects of mother–infant singing on emotional closeness, affect, anxiety, and stress hormones. Music & Science, 1.

Loewy J., Stewart K., Dassler A.-M., Telsey A., Homel P. (2013). The effects of music therapy on vital signs, feeding, and sleep in premature infants. Pediatrics. 131(5):902–918.

Markova G., Nguyen T., Schätz C., de Eccher M. (2020). Singing in tune – being in tune: relationship between maternal playful singing and interpersonal synchrony. Enfance. 1(1):89–107.

Mehr S.A., Song L.A., Spelke E.S. (2016). For 5-month-old infants, melodies are social. Psychol. Sci. 27(4):486–501.

Milligan K., Atkinson L., Trehub S.E., Benoit D., Poulton L. (2003). Maternal attachment and the communication of emotion through song. Infant Behav. Dev. 26(1):1–13.

Nagy, E., Cosgrove, R., Robertson, N., Einhoff, T. and Orvos, H. (2022). Neonatal Musicality: Do Newborns Detect Emotions in Music? Psychological Studies, 67(4), pp.501–513.

Trainor L.J. (1996). Infant preferences for infant-directed versus noninfant-directed playsongs and lullabies. Infant Behav. Dev. 19(1):83–92.

Trehub, S.E. (2019). Nurturing infants with music. International Journal of Music in Early Childhood, 14(1), pp.9–15.

Tsang C.D., Falk S., Hessel A. (2017). Infants prefer infant-directed song over speech. Child Dev. 88(4):1207–1215.

Nagy, E., Cosgrove, R., Robertson, N., Einhoff, T. and Orvos, H. (2022). Neonatal Musicality: Do Newborns Detect Emotions in Music? Psychological Studies, 67(4), pp.501–513.

Nakata T., Trehub S.E. (2004). Infants' responsiveness to maternal speech and singing. Infant Behav. Dev. 27(4):455–464.

Anbalagan, S., Velasquez, J.H., Staufert Gutierrez, D., Devagiri, S., Nieto, D. and Ankola, P. (2023). Music for pain relief of minor procedures in term neonates. Pediatric Research, pp.1–5.

Ball, Helen, L. (2007). Together or apart? A behavioural and physiological investigation of sleeping arrangements for twin babies, Midwifery, Volume 23, Issue 4, Pages 404-412, ISSN 0266-6138

Klein, B. (2020). New Understandings of Twin Relationships: From Harmony to Estrangement and Loneliness

Nyqvist, Kerstin Hedberg Lutes, Linda M. (1998). Co-bedding Twins: A Developmentally Supportive Care Strategy, Journal of Obstetric, Gynecologic & Neonatal Nursing, Volume 27, Issue 4, Pages 450-456, ISSN 0884-2175,

Thomas, J.G. (1996). The Early Parenting of Twins. Military Medicine, 161(4), pp.233–235.

Addyman, C., & Addyman, I. (2013). The science of baby laughter. Comedy Studies, 4(2), 143–153.

Hoicka, E., Telli, B.S., Prouten, E., Leckie, G., Browne, W.J., Mireault, G. and Fox, C. (2021). The Early Humor Survey (EHS): A reliable parent-report measure of humor development for 1- to 47-month-olds. Behavior Research Methods.

Mireault, G. C., Crockenberg, S. C., Sparrow, J. E., Cousineau, K., Pettinato, C., & Woodard, K. (2015). Laughing matters: Infant humor in the context of parental affect. Journal of experimental child psychology, 136, 30–41.

Sroufe A, Wunsch J. (1972). The development of laughter in the first year of life. Child Development. 43:1326–1344.

An, M., Marcinowski, E.C., Hsu, L.-Y., Stankus, J., Jancart, K.L., Lobo, M.A., Dusing, S.C., McCoy, S.W., Bovaird, J.A., Willett, S. and Harbourne, R.T. (2022). Object Permanence and the Relationship to Sitting Development in Infants With Motor Delays. Pediatric Physical Therapy, 34(3), pp.309–316.

Parrott, W.G. and Gleitman, H. (1989). Infants' Expectations in Play: The Joy of Peek-a-boo. Cognition and Emotion, 3(4), pp.291–311.

Wood, K. (2001). Stages of Cognitive Development," in Orey, M. Emerging Perspectives on Learning, Teaching, and Technology, Association for

Educational Communications and Technology

Marques-Bruna P, Grimshaw PN. (1998). Variability in development of overarm throwing: a longitudinal case study over the first 6 months of throwing. Percept Mot Skills. 86(3 Pt 2):1403-18.

Gerber, Magda; Greenwald, Deborah; Weaver, Joan, eds. (2013). The RIE Manual for parents and professionals (2nd ed.). Los Angeles, CA: Resources for Infant Educarers (RIE).

Harrison, Y. (2004). The relationship between daytime exposure to light and night-time sleep in 6-12-week-old infants. Journal of Sleep Research, 13(4), pp.345–352.

Hart, J.L., & Tannock, M.T. (2013). Playful aggression in early childhood settings. Children Australia, 38(3), 106-114

Paquette, D., Carbonneau, R., Dubeau, D., Bigras, M. & Tremblay, R.E. (2003). Prevalence of father-child rough-and-tumble play and physical aggression in preschool children. European Journal of Psychology of Education, 18, 171-1

Brooker, R.J., Buss, K.A., Lemery-Chalfant, K., Aksan, N., Davidson, R.J. and Goldsmith, H.H. (2013). The development of stranger fear in infancy and toddlerhood: normative development, individual differences, antecedents, and outcomes. Developmental Science, 16(6), p.n/a-n/a.

Field T. (2008). Problems in infancy. In: Hersen M, Gross AM, editors. Handbook of Clinical Psychology. Vol. 2. Hoboken, NJ: John Wiley & Sons. pp. 966–1011. Children and Adolescents.

Griggs, J., Tan, J.-P., Buchanan, A., Attar-Schwartz, S. and Flouri, E. (2009). 'They've Always Been There For Me': Grandparental Involvement and Child Well-Being. Children & Society. APA Dictionary of Psychology. Stranger Anxiety.

Van Hulle CA, Moore MN, Lemery-Chalfant K, et al. (2017). Infant stranger fear trajectories predict anxious behaviors and diurnal cortisol rhythm during childhood. Development and Psychopathology. 29(3):1119-1130.

Busman R. Separation Anxiety: What Parents Should Know. Anxiety and Depression Association of America.

Brooker RJ, Buss KA, Lemery-Chalfant K, et al. (2013). The development of stranger fear in infancy and toddlerhood: normative development, individual differences, antecedents, and outcomes. Developmental Science. 16(6):864-878.

Ryu H, Han G, Choi J, et al. (2017). Object permanence and the development of attention capacity in preterm and term infants: an eye-tracking study. Italian Journal of Pediatrics. 43:90.

Colonnesi, C., Stams, G. J. J., Koster, I., & Noom, M. J. (2010). The relation between pointing and language development: A meta-analysis. Developmental Review, 30, 352-366

Lüke, C., Ritterfeld, U., Grimminger, A., Liszkowski, U., & Rohlfing, K. J. (2017). Development of pointing gestures in children with typical and delayed language acquisition. Journal of Speech, Language, and Hearing Research, 60, 3185-3197

Edalati, M., Wallois, F., Safaie, J., Ghostine, G., Kongolo, G., Trainor, L.J., Moghimi, S. (2023). Rhythm in the premature neonate brain: Very early processing of auditory beat and meter. The Journal of Neuroscience, JN-RM-1100–22. 10.1523/JNEUROSCI.1100-22.2023

Gábor P. Háden, Fleur L. Bouwer, Henkjan Honing, István Winkler (2024). Beat processing in newborn infants cannot be explained by statistical learning based on transition probabilities, Cognition, Volume 243, 105670, ISSN 0010-0277

Ho, P., Tsao, J.C.I., Bloch, L. and Zeltzer, L.K. (2011). The Impact of Group Drumming on Social-Emotional Behavior in Low-Income Children. Evidence-Based Complementary and Alternative Medicine, 2011, pp.1–14.

Kim, M., & Schachner, A. (2023). The origins of dance: Characterizing the development of infants' earliest dance behavior. Developmental Psychology, 59(4), 691–706.

Nguyen, T., Flaten, E., Trainor, L. J., & Novembre, G. (2023). Early social communication through music: State of the art and future perspectives. Developmental Cognitive Neuroscience, 63, 1–14.

Krol, K.M. and Grossmann, T. (2018). Psychological effects of breastfeeding on children and mothers. Bundesgesundheitsblatt - Gesundheitsforschung - Gesundheitsschutz, 61(8), pp.977–985.

Modak, A., Ronghe, V. and Gomase, K.P. (2023). The Psychological Benefits of Breastfeeding: Fostering Maternal Well-Being and Child Development. Cureus, 15(10).

Chapter 3: Your 12–18-month-old

Field T, Hernandez-Reif M, Vera Y, Gil K, Diego M, Sanders C. (2005). Infants of depressed mothers facing a mirror versus their mother. Infant Behavior and Development. c;28:48–53

Garafova, A., Romanova, Z., Henrieta Oravcova, et al. (2023). Bridging the mood and stress hormone levels between mothers and their babies: The study design and first preliminary results. Acta psychologica, 238, pp.103977–103977.

Gerhardt, S. (2014). Why Love Matters: How affection shapes a baby's brain, Routledge

Hernandez-Reif M, Field T, Diego M, Vera Y, Pickens J. (2006). Happy faces are habituated more slowly by infants of depressed mothers. Infant Behavior & Development. c;29:131–35.

Waters SF, West TV, Karnilowicz HR, Mendes WB. (2017). Affect contagion between mothers and infants: Examining valence and touch. J Exp Psychol Gen. 146(7):1043-1051.

Begus K, Gliga T, Southgate V. (2014). Infants learn what they want to learn: responding to infant pointing leads to superior learning. PLoS One. 9(10):e108817. d

Diessel, H. (2006). Demonstratives, joint attention, and the emergence of grammar. Cognitive Linguistics, 17(4).

Hsu HC, Iyer SN. Early gesture, early vocabulary, and risk of language impairment in preschoolers. Res Dev Disabil. 57:201-10

Kovács ÁM, Tauzin T, Téglás E, Gergely G, Csibra G. (2014). Pointing as Epistemic Request: 12-month-olds Point to Receive New Information. Infanc. 19(6):543-557

Tamis-LeMonda CS, Kuchirko, Y, and Song L. (2014). Why is infant language learning facilitated by parental responsiveness? Curr. Dir. Psychol. Sci. 23: 121–126

Lillard, A. S., Lerner, M. D., Hopkins, E. J., Dore, R. A., Smith, E. D., & Palmquist, C. M. (2013). The impact of pretend play on children's development: A review of the evidence. Psychological bulletin, 139(1), 1-34

Vygotsky, L. S. (1978). The Role of Play in Development. In Mind in Society. (pp. 92-104). Cambridge, MA: Harvard University Press

Whitebread, D., Neale, D., Jensen, H., Liu, C., Solis, S., Hopkins, E., Hirsh-Pasek, K. and Zosh, J. (2017). The role of play in children's development: a review of the evidence White paper.

Liquin E.G., Lombrozo T. (2020). Explanation-seeking curiosity in childhood. Curr Opin Behav Sci.;35:14–20

Shah P.E., Weeks H.M., Richards B., Kaciroti N. (2018). Early childhood curiosity and kindergarten reading and math academic achievement. Pediatr Res. 84:380–386.

Von Stumm S., Hell B., Chamorro-Premuzic T. (2011). The hungry mind: intellectual curiosity is the third pillar of academic performance. Perspect Psychol Sci. 6:574–588.

Alberini, C. M. & Travaglia, A. (2017). Infantile amnesia: A critical period of learning to learn and remember. J Neurosci 37, 5783– 5795

Akers, K. G. et al (2014). Hippocampal neurogenesis regulates forgetting during adulthood and infancy. Science 344, 598– 602

Bauer, P.J. (1996). What do infants recall of their lives? Memory for specific events by one- to two-year-olds. American Psychologist, 51(1), pp.29–41.

Hayne, H., MacDonald, S., & Barr, R. (1997).Developmental changes in the specificity of

memory over the second year of life. Infant Behavior and Development, 20, 233–245

Uchihara, T., Webb, S. & Yanagisawa, A. (2019). The Effects of Repetition on Incidental Vocabulary Learning: A Meta-Analysis of Correlational Studies. Language Learning, 69 (3): 559 – 599

Spencer, J.P. (2020). The Development of Working Memory. Current Directions in Psychological Science, 29(6), pp.545–553.

Reese, E., Macfarlane, L., McAnally, H., Robertson, S.-J. and Taumoepeau, M. (2020). Coaching in maternal reminiscing with preschoolers leads to elaborative and coherent personal narratives in early adolescence. Journal of Experimental Child Psychology, 189, p.104707.

Squire, L. R. & Dede, A. J. O. (2015). Conscious and unconscious memory systems. Cold Spring Harb Perspect Biol 7, a021667

Arterberry, M., & Bornstein, M. (2001). Three-month-old infants' categorization of animals and vehicles based on static and dynamic attributes. Journal of Experimental Child Psychology, 80, 333–346

Lane, J.D., Wellman, H.M. and Evans, E.M. (2010). Children's understanding of ordinary and extraordinary minds. Child Development 81(5), 1475–1489

DeLoache, J. S., Pickard, M. B., & LoBue, V. (2011). How very young children think about animals. In P. McCardle, S. McCune, J. A. Griffin, & V. Maholmes (Eds.), How animals affect us: Examining the influences of human–animal interaction on child development and human health (pp. 85–99). American Psychological Association.

Lieven EV, Pine JM, Barnes HD. (1992). Individual differences in early vocabulary development: redefining the referential-expressive distinction. J Child Lang. 19(2):287-310.

Melson, G. F. (1987). The role of pets in the development of children's nurturance. Paper presented to the annual meeting of the Delta Society

Minatoya, M., Ikeda-Araki, A., Miyashita, C., Itoh, S., Kobayashi, S., Yamazaki, K., Ait Bamai, Y., Saijo, Y., Sato, Y., Ito, Y. and Kishi, R. (2021). Association between Early Life Child Development and Family Dog Ownership: A Prospective Birth Cohort Study of the Japan Environment and Children's Study. International Journal of Environmental Research and Public Health, 18(13), p.7082.

Poresky, R. H. and Hendrix, C. (1990). Developmental benefits of pets for young children. Paper presented at the Delta Society 7th Annual Conference

Reddy, R.B., Echelbarger, M., Toomajian, N., Hammond, T. and Wellman, H.M. (2023). Do children help dogs spontaneously? Human-Animal Interactions

Wedl, M. and Kotrschal, K. (2009). Social and Individual Components of Animal Contact in Preschool Children. Anthrozoös, 22(4), pp.383–396.

Kidd, C. and Hayden, Benjamin Y. (2015). The Psychology and Neuroscience of Curiosity. Neuron, 88(3), pp.449–460.

Oudeyer, P.-Y. and Smith, L.B. (2016). How Evolution May Work Through Curiosity-Driven Developmental Process. Topics in Cognitive Science, 8(2), pp.492–502.

Wright, J.S. and Panksepp, J. (2012). An Evolutionary Framework to Understand Foraging, Wanting, and Desire: The Neuropsychology of the SEEKING System. Neuropsychoanalysis, 14(1), pp.5–39.

Adair S. M. (2003). Pacifier use in children: a review of recent literature. Pediatr. Dent. 25, 449–458. PMID:

Alcock K., Connor S. (2021). Oral motor and gesture abilities independently associated with preschool language skill: longitudinal and concurrent relationships at 21 months and 3–4 years. J. Speech Lang. Hear. Res. 64, 1944–1963.

Barca L., Mazzuca C., Borghi A. M. (2017). Pacifier overuse and conceptual relations of abstract and emotional concepts. Front. Psychol. 8:2014.

Elserafy, F.A., Alsaedi, S.A., Louwrens, J., Bin Sadiq, B. and Mersal, A.Y. (2009). Oral sucrose and a pacifier for pain relief during simple procedures in preterm infants: a randomized controlled trial. Annals of Saudi medicine, 29(3), pp.184–8.

Gederi A., Coomaraswamy K., Turner P. J. (2013). Pacifiers: a review of risks vs benefits. Dent. Update 40, 92–101.

Strutt C., Khattab G., Willoughby J. (2021). Does the duration and frequency of dummy (pacifier) use affect the development of speech? Int. J. Lang. Commun. Disord. 56, 512–527.

Tsao F. M., Liu H. M., Kuhl P. K. (2004). Speech perception in infancy predicts language development in the second year of life: a longitudinal study. Child Dev. 75, 1067–1084.

Winnicott DW: (1951). Transitional objects and transitional phenomena. Through Pediatrics to Psychoanalysis. London: Hogarth Press

Mallan, K.M., Jansen, E., Harris, H., Llewellyn, C., Fildes, A., & Daniels, L.A. (2018). Feeding a fussy eater: Examining longitudinal bidirectional relationships between child fussy eating and maternal feeding practices. Journal of Pediatric Psychology, 43(10), 1138-1146.

Taylor, C.M., Wernimont, S.M., Northstone, K., & Emmett, P.M. (2015). Picky/fussy eating in children: Review of definitions, assessment, prevalence and dietary intakes. Appetite, 95, 349-359.

Verhage, C.L., Gillebaart, M., van der Veek, S.M.C., & Vereijken, C.M.J.L. (2018). The relation between family meals and health of infants and toddlers: A review. Appetite, 127, 97-109.

Wolstenholme, H., Heary, C., & Kelly, C. (2019). Fussy eating behaviours: Response patterns in families of school-aged children. Appetite, 136, 93-102.

Adolph KE, & Tamis-LeMonda CS. (2014). The costs and benefits of development: The transition from crawling to walking. Child Development Perspectives 8: 187–192.

Clearfield MW. (2011). Learning to walk changes infants' social interactions. Infant Behavior and Development, 34(1), 15–25

De Bartolo, D., Zandvoort, C.S., Goudriaan, M., Kerkman, J.N., Iosa, M. and Dominici, N. (2022). The Role of Walking Experience in the Emergence of Gait Harmony in Typically Developing Toddlers. Brain Sciences, 12(2), p.155.

Hospodar, C.M., Hoch, J.E., Lee, D.K., Shrout, P.E. and Adolph, K.E. (2021). Practice and proficiency: Factors that facilitate infant walking skill. Developmental Psychobiology, 63(7).

Lynn T. Staheli (2006). "Shoes", Practice of pediatric orthopedics, Lippincott Williams & Wilkins, p. 47, ISBN 978-1-58255-818-9

Liu W, Mei Q, Yu P, Gao Z, Hu Q, Fekete G, et al. (2022). Biomechanical Characteristics of the Typically Developing Toddler Gait: A Narrative Review. Children (Basel, Switzerland). 9(3):406

Nuñez-Lisboa, M., Bastien, G., Schepens, B., Lacquaniti, F., Ivanenko, Y.P. and Dewolf, A.H. (2023). Effect of age and speed on the step-to-step transition strategies in children. Journal of Biomechanics, 157, pp.111704–111704.

Walle EA & Campos JJ. (2014). Infant language development is related to the acquisition of walking. Developmental Psychology 50: 336–348

Feiman R., Mody S., Sanborn S., Carey S. (2017). What do you mean, no? Toddlers' comprehension of logical "no" and "not". Lang. Learn. Dev. 13 430–450. 10.1080/15475441.2017.1317253

Gerber, M. (2012). Your Self–Confident Baby: How to Encourage Your Child's Natural Abilities — From the Very Start, John Wiley & Sons

Guidetti, M. (2005). Yes or no? How do young children combine gestures and words to agree and refuse. Journal of Child Language, 32, 911–924.

Hoyniak CP, Bates JE, McQuillan ME, Albert LE, Staples AD, Molfese VJ, Rudasill KM, Deater-Deckard K. (2021). The Family Context of Toddler Sleep: Routines, Sleep Environment, and Emotional Security Induction in the Hour before Bedtime. Behav Sleep Med. 19(6):795-813.

Diesendruck, G. and Perez, R. (2015). Toys are me: Children's extension of self to objects. Cognition, 134, pp.11–20.

Litt, C.J. (1986). Theories of Transitional Object Attachment: An Overview. International Journal of Behavioral Development, 9(3), pp.383–399.

Li, M., Wang, D., Xu, W., & Mao, Z. (Eddie). (2017). Motivation for family vacations with young children: anecdotes from the Internet. Journal of Travel & Tourism Marketing, 34(8), 1047–1057.

McCarthy, L., Delbosc, A., Currie, G., & Molloy, A. (2017). Factors influencing travel mode choice among families with young children (aged 0–4): a review of the literature. Transport Reviews, 37(6), 767–781.

Price, Laura, Matthews, Bryan. (2013).Travel time as quality time: parental attitudes to long distance travel with young children, Journal of Transport Geography, Volume 32, Pages 49-55, ISSN 0966-6923,

Acevedo, B.P., Aron, E.N., Aron, A., Sangster, M.-D., Collins, N. and Brown, L.L. (2014). The highly sensitive brain: an fMRI study of sensory processing sensitivity and response to others' emotions. Brain and Behavior, 4(4), pp.580–594.

Aron, E.N (2002). The Highly Sensitive Child, The Highly Sensitive Child: Helping Our Children Thrive When the World Overwhelms Them, Harmony Books

Assary E., Zavos H., Krapohl E., Keers R., Pluess M. (2020). Genetic architecture of Environmental Sensitivity reflects multiple heritable components: A twin study with adolescents. Mol. Psychiatry. 1–9.

Lionetti F., Aron A., Aron E.N., Burns G.L., Jagiellowicz J., Pluess M. (2018). Dandelions, tulips and orchids: Evidence for the existence of low-sensitive, medium-sensitive and high-sensitive individuals. Transl. Psychiatry. 8:24.

Horst, J. S., Parsons, K. L., and Bryan, N. M. (2011). Get the story straight: contextual repetition promotes word learning from storybooks. Front. Psychol. 2:17.

Kidd, D.C. and Castano, E. (2013). Reading Literary Fiction Improves Theory of Mind. Science, 342(6156), pp.377–380.

Sénéchal, M. (1997). The differential effect of storybook reading on preschoolers' acquisition of expressive and receptive vocabulary. J. Child Lang. 24, 123–138

Kellogg, R. (1970). Analysing Children's Art (Palo Alto, California, National Press)

Lewis, D. & Greene, J. (1983). Your Child's Drawings ... their hidden meaning (London, Hutchinson)

Chapter 4: Your 18–24 month-old

Brownell, C.A., Iesue, S.S., Nichols, S.R. and Svetlova, M. (2012). Mine or Yours? Development of Sharing in Toddlers in Relation to Ownership Understanding. Child Development, 84(3), pp.906–920.

Chernyak N and Kushnir T. (2013). "Giving pre- schoolers choice increases sharing behaviour", Psychological Science 24, no. 10, pp1971–1979

Bryan, J. H. and London, P. (1970). "Altruistic behaviour in children", Psychological Bulletin 73, no. 3, pp200–211

O'Brien L, Murray R. (2007). Forest School and its impacts on young children: Case studies in Britain. Urban Forestry and Urban Greening, 6, pp. 249-265

Warren SF, Rogers-Warren A and Baer DM. (1976), "The role of offer rates in controlling sharing by young children", Journal of Applied Behaviour Analysis 9, no. 4, pp491–497

Weinstein, N, Przybylski, A.K. Ryan, R.M. (2009). Can nature make us more caring? Effects of immersion in nature on intrinsic aspirations and generosity. Personality and Social Psychology Bulletin, 35, pp. 1315-1329

Hashmi, S., Vanderwert, R. E., Paine, A. L., & Gerson, S. A. (2022). Doll play prompts social thinking and social talking: Representations of internal state language in the brain. Developmental Science, 25, e13163.

Foulkes, D. (1990). Dreaming and consciousness. European Journal of Cognitive Psychology, 2(1), pp.39–55.

Harris, P. L. , German, T. , & Mills, P. (1996). Children's use of counterfactual thinking in causal reasoning. Cognition, 61, 233–259

Piaget, J. (1952). Play, dreams and imitation in childhood. W W Norton & Co

Singer, D.G., & J.L. Singer (1990). The house of make-believe: Children's

play and the developing imagination. Cambridge, MA: Harvard University Press

Weisberg, D. S. , & Gopnik, A. (2013). Pretense, counterfactuals, and Bayesian causal models: Why what is not real really matters. Cognitive Science, 37(7), 1368–1381. 10.1111/cogs.12069

Qian, G., Li, R., Yang, W., Li, R., Tian, L., & Dou, G. (2021). Sibling jealousy and temperament: The mediating effect of emotion regulation in China during COVID-19 pandemic. Frontiers in Psychiatry, 12, 729883.

Volling, B.L., Oh, W., Gonzalez, R., Bader, L.R., Tan, L., & Rosenberg, L. (2021). Changes in children's attachment security to mother and father after the birth of a sibling: Risk and resilience in the family. Development and Psychopathology, 35(3), 1404-1420.

Hart, S. and Carrington, H. (2002). Jealousy in 6-Month-Old Infants. Infancy, 3(3), pp.395–402.

Miller, A.L., Volling, B.L. and McElwain, N.L. (2000). Sibling jealousy in a triadic context with mothers and fathers. Review of Social Development, 9(4), pp.433–457.

Dahl A., Freda G. F. (2017). "How young children come to view harming others as wrong: a developmental analysis," in Social Cognition. eds. Sommerville J. A., Decety J. (London: Routledge;), 151–184

Davidov M, Grusec J. E. (2006). Untangling the links of parental responsiveness to distress and warmth to child outcomes. Child Dev. 77, 44–58.

Decety, Jean, and Kalina J. Michalska (2010). "Neurodevelopmental changes in the circuits underlying empathy and sympathy from childhood to adulthood." Developmental science 13.6: 886-899

Denham, SA, Mitchell-Copeland J, Strandberg K, Auerbach S and Blair K. (1997). Parental contributions to preschoolers' emotional competence: Direct and indirect effects. Motivation and Emotion 21:65–86

Farrant B. M., Devine T. A. J., Maybery M. T., Fletcher J. (2012). Empathy, perspective taking and prosocial behaviour: the importance of parenting practices. Infant Child Dev. 21, 175–188.

Mikulincer, M., Shaver, P. R., Gillath, O., & Nitzberg, R. A. (2005). Attachment, Caregiving, and Altruism: Boosting Attachment Security Increases Compassion and Helping. Journal of Personality and Social Psychology, 89(5), 817-839

Panfile T. M., Laible D. J. (2012). Attachment security and child's empathy: the mediating role of emotion regulation. Merrill Palmer Q. 58, 1–21.

Santelices, M.-P. et al. (2022). 'Keeping Children in Mind: Mentalizing Capacities of Caregivers and Educators and the Development of Theory of Mind in Preschool Children', Trends in Psychology [Preprint].

Simner M. L. (1971). Newborn's response to the cry of another infant. Dev. Psychol. 5, 136–150.

Strayer J., Roberts W. (2004). Children's anger, emotional expressiveness, and empathy: relations with parents' empathy, emotional expressiveness, and parenting practices. Soc. Dev. 13, 229–254.

Zahn-Waxler C., Radke-Yarrow M., Wagner E., Chapman M. (1992). Development of concern for others. Dev. Psychol. 28, 126–136.

Berkowitz L. (1989). Frustration-aggression hypothesis: Examination and reformulation. Psychological Bulletin. 106(1):59–73.

Lamb S. (1991). First moral sense: Aspects of and contributors to a beginning morality in the second year of life. In: Kurtines WM, Gewirtz JL, editors. Handbook of moral behavior and development. Vol. 2: Research. Hillsdale, NJ: Lawrence Erlbaum Associates, Inc. pp. 171–190

Adams RJ, Courage ML, Mercer ME. (1991). Deficiencies in human neonates' color vision: photoreceptoral and neural explanations. Behav Brain Res. 43(2):109-14

Goulart PR, Bandeira ML, Tsubota D, Oiwa NN, Costa MF, Ventura DF. (2008). A computer-controlled color vision test for children based on the Cambridge Colour Test. Vis Neurosci. 25(3):445-50

Kowalski, K., & Zimiles, H. (2006). The relation between children's conceptual functioning with color and color term acquisition. Journal of Experimental Child Psychology, 94(4), 301-321

O'Hanlon, C.G., and Roberson, D. (2006). Learning in context: Linguistic and attentional constraints on children's color term learning. Journal of Experimental Child Psychology, 94(4): 275-300

Ramscar, M., Yarlett, D., Dye, M., Denny, K., & Thorpe, K. (2010). The effects of feature label order and their implications for symbolic learning. Cognitive Science, 34(6), 909-957

Blum, N.J., Taubman, B. and Nemeth, N. (2003). Relationship Between Age at Initiation of Toilet Training and Duration of Training: A Prospective Study. PEDIATRICS, 111(4), pp.810–814.

Wyndaele, J.-J., Kaerts, N., Wyndaele, M. and Vermandel, A. (2020). Development Signs in Healthy Toddlers in Different Stages of Toilet Training: Can They Help Define Readiness and Probability of Success? Global Pediatric Health, 7, p.2333794X2095108.

Bender JM, Lee Y, Ryoo JH, Boucke L, Sun M, Ball TS, Rugolotto S, She RC. (2021). A Longitudinal Study of Assisted Infant Toilet Training During the First Year of Life. J Dev Behav Pediatr. 42(8):648-655

Cirelli L.K., Trehub S.E., Trainor L.J. (2018). Rhythm and melody as social signals for infants. Ann. N. Y. Acad. Sci.

Kim, M., & Schachner, A. (2022). The origins of dance: Characterizing the development of infants' earliest dance behavior. Developmental Psychology.

Kirschner, S., & Tomasello, M. (2010). Joint music making promotes prosocial behavior in 4-year-old children. Evolution and Human Behavior, 31(5), 354–364.

Nguyen, T., Flaten, E., Trainor, L.J. and Novembre, G. (2023). Early social communication through music: State of the art and future perspectives. Developmental Cognitive Neuroscience, 63, pp.101279–101279.

Antell, S. E., & Keating, D. P. (1983). Perception of numerical invariance in neonates. Child Development, 54(3), 695–701.

Jordan, N. C., Levine, S. C., & Huttenlocher, J. (1994). Development of calculation abilities in middle- and low-income children after formal instruction in school. Journal of Applied Developmental Psychology, 15(2), 223–240.

Fernald A, Zangl R, Portillo AL, Marchman VA. (2008). Looking while listening: Using eye movements to monitor spoken language comprehension by infants and young children. In: Sekerina IA, Fernandez EM, Clahsen H, editors. Developmental Psycholinguistics: On-line methods in children's language processing. J. Benjamins Pub.; Amsterdam; Philadelphia

Hutton, J.S., Dudley, J., Horowitz-Kraus, T., DeWitt, T. and Holland, S.K. (2020). Associations Between Screen-Based Media Use and Brain White Matter Integrity in Preschool-Aged Children. JAMA Pediatrics, 174(1), p.e193869.

Marchman VA, Fernald A. (2008). Speed of word recognition and vocabulary knowledge in infancy predict cognitive and language outcomes in later childhood. Developmental Science. 11:F9–16

Weisleder, A. and Fernald, A. (2013). Talking to Children matters: Early Language Experience Strengthens Processing and Builds Vocabulary. Psychological Science, 24(11), pp.2143–2152.

Akhtar N, Menjivar JA. (2012). Cognitive and linguistic correlates of early exposure to more than one language. In: Benson JB, editor. Advances in child development and behavior. Vol. 42. Burlington: Academic Press. pp. 41–78

Bedore LM, Peña ED. (2008). Assessment of bilingual children for identification of language impairment: Current findings and implications for practice. International Journal of Bilingual Education and Bilingualism. 11(1):1–29.

Bialystok E, Craik FIM, Luk G. Bilingualism (2012). consequences for mind and brain. Trends in Cognitive Sciences. 16(4):240–250.

Kovacs, A., & Mehler, J. (2009). Cognitive gains in 7-month-old bilingual infants. Proceedings of the National Academy of Sciences, 106 (16), 6556-6560

Hoff, E., & Core, C. (2013). Input and language development in bilingually developing children. Seminars in Speech and Language, 34(4), 215-226

Blum-Ross, Alicia and Livingstone, Sonia (2016). Families and screen time: current advice and emerging research. LSE Media Policy Project, Media Policy Brief 17. The London School of Economics and Political Science, London, UK

Hirsh-Pasek, K., Zosh, J. M., Golinkoff, R. M., Gray, J. H., Robb, M. B., and Kaufman, J. (2015). Putting education in educational apps: Lessons from the science of learning. Psychol. Sci. 16, 3–34.

Van den Heuvel, M., Ma, J., Borkhoff, C. M., Koroshegyi, C., Dai, D., Parkin, P., et al. (2019). Mobile media device use is associated with expressive language delay in 18-month-old children. Dev. Behav. Pediatr. 40, 99–104.

Zimmerman FJ, Christakis DA, Meltzoff AN. (2007). Associations between media viewing and language development in children under age 2 years. J Pediatr. 151(4):364-8.

Eaton, W. O., & Enns, L. R. (1986). Sex differences in human motor activity level. Psychological Bulletin, 100(1), 19–28.

Hines M. (2010). Sex-related variation in human behavior and the brain. Trends Cogn Sci. 14(10):448-56.

Kuzawa, C.W., Chugani, H.T., Grossman, L.I., Lipovich, L., Muzik, O., Hof, P.R., Wildman, D.E., Sherwood, C.C., Leonard, W.R. and Lange, N. (2014). Metabolic costs and evolutionary implications of human brain development. Proceedings of the National Academy of Sciences, 111(36), pp.13010–13015.

AACAP (2020). Screen Time and Children. Aacap.org. https://www.aacap.org/AACAP/Families_and_Youth/Facts_for_Families/FFF-Guide/Children-And-Watching-TV-054.asp

Christakis DA, Gilkerson J, Richards JA, et al. (2009). Audible television and decreased adult words, infant vocalizations, and conversational turns: a population-based study. Arch Pediatr Adolesc Med. 163(6):554-558.

Madigan S, et al. (2020). Associations between screen use and child language skills: A systematic review and meta-analysis. JAMA Pediatrics.

INDEX

A
adrenaline 28, 57
   aggression
      new siblings 162–63, 166–67
      to others 170–71
amygdala 12
animals 73, 122–23, 160, 161
arguments 40, 41
arms, flexing 31, 35
attachment 17, 50
attention 11
autonomy 15

B
babbling 16, 17, 21, 72–73
baby gyms 31, 59
babysitters 124–25
balance 74
banging 102–03
bath time 76–77
bedtime routines 57, 137
behaviour, modelling 9
bilingualism 190–91
birthdays 150–51
birth trauma 33
biting 170–71, 173
body language
   newborns 31
   sense of safety 111
bonding 20–21, 29, 66–67, 121
books 144–45, 197
boredom, crying 53
bottle feeding 43
boundaries
   setting 9, 170
   testing 104, 121, 134
brain
   changes for mother 22
   development overview 12–13, 19
   feedback loops 30
   memory 15, 101, 118–19
breastfeeding
   after food is introduced 106–07
   hormones 106
   latching on 37
   parent recognition 29
   responsive feeding 43
   sleeping 49
   stopping 107
brushing teeth 178–79
button pressing 126–27

C
caregiving
   childcare providers 124–25, 143, 158–59
   other trusted people 51, 124
   stranger anxiety 98–99
   swapping roles 41
   taking turns 23, 40, 89
carrying, slings 35, 163
cause and effect 14, 18, 47, 94, 126, 134, 149
cerebral cortex 12
childcare providers 124–25, 143, 158–59
choking 79
Christmas 150–51
circadian rhythms 54–55
clapping 102–03
coats, refusing to wear 176–77
colours 180–81
comfort objects 18, 128–29, 138–39
communication *see also* speech
   crying 52–53
   gaze 29
   laughter 90–91
   non-verbal 111
   pointing 83, 100–101
   relationships 23, 40, 41
   smiling 50, 51, 62–63
concentration 115, 117
connection *see* bonding
contentment 8
co-parenting 23, 40–41, 89, 111, 120–21, 140
co-regulation 20
corpus callosum 13
cortisol 28, 37, 52, 57
co-sleeping 48–49, 88
counselling, premature birth 33
crawling 80–81
cross-eyes 59
crying
   naming emotions 129
   newborns 52–53
   new siblings 163, 166
   night waking 56
curiosity 14–15, 18, 116–17, 126–27, 174–75
cutlery 79

D
dancing 184–85
development overview
   0–6 months 16
   6–12 months 17
   12–18 months 18
   18–24 months 19
doors, opening and closing 117
dopamine 37, 93, 116
drawing 148–49
dreams 161
dropping food 94–95
drumming 102–03
dummies 128–29

E
ears *see also* hearing
   sensitivity 39
   vestibular system 74
echolalia 19
emotions
   brain development 12
   hormones 16
   memory 119
   naming 9, 143, 167, 169
   parenting 9, 11, 23
   safety 28
   sensitivity 142–43
   toddlers understanding parents 168–69
   understanding 9, 21
energy levels 194–95
experience, learning from 14
eyes *see also* sight
   colour blindness 181
   newborns 26–27
   squints 59

F
faces, funny faces 51
falls 132
fathers, hormone changes 22
feeding
   circadian rhythms 55
   growth spurts 42
   newborns 36–37, 42–43
   night-time 37, 54
   reflexes 36, 37, 43, 45
   sight development 27

feet
  crawling 81
  walking 133
fight-or-flight response 34, 171
finance 41
fingers, sucking 29, 31, 70
flying games 74–75
focus 15
food
  dropping 94–95
  eating locations 71
  fibre 183
  grazing 131
  introducing 78–79
  portion sizes 130, 131
  sugar levels 195
  toddlers refusing 130–31
formula milk see bottle feeding
friends 156–57

G
gagging 79
games see play
gas, body language 31
grandparents 99
grasp reflex 16, 44–45
Green Cross Code 147
growth spurts 42

H
hair-washing 178–79
hands
  fine motor skills 101
  pincer grasp 17, 70
  pointing 83, 100–101
  scribbling 148–49
head, neck strength 58
hearing 38–39 see also sound
heartbeat, parent's 57
help, asking for 9, 22, 41, 111
hide-and-seek 93, 125
hippocampus 118
hitting 170–71, 173
holding 8, 29, 110
hormones
  bonding 20
  breastfeeding 106
  emotions 16
  hunger 37
  laughter 90
  senses and learning 28
  sleep 55, 57
  stress 28, 52
hunger
  crawling 80
  crying 53
  cues 37, 42–43
  toddlers 131

I
imagination 114, 151, 157, 160–61
imitation 21, 47, 62–63
immune system 70
independence 104, 120, 130, 134, 176
Internal Working Model 21

J
jealousy 166–67
joint attention 100
journeys 140–41

K
kangaroo care 33

L
labels, not using 8, 111
language see speech
laughter 90–91
learning 14–15, 97
legs, flexing 31, 35
let's pretend games see role-playing
letters, learning 187
light levels
  body clock 55
  overstimulation 31, 53
  sight development 27
limbic system 12
lullabies 86, 87

M
massage 33, 67
melatonin 55, 57
memory 15, 101, 118–19, 151
mess 116–17
mirroring 21, 63, 91
mirrors, recognition of self 84–85
modelling 157, 182
money 41
Moro reflex 34–35
mothers, brain changes 22
motor cortex, feedback loop 30
motor skills 101, 118
mouthing 70–71
movement
  autonomy 15
  balance and gravity 74
  crawling 80–81
  development overview 16–19
  energy levels 194–95
  flying games 74–75
  newborns 30–31
  rolling over 64–65
  walking 132–33
music 61, 184–85
myelin 13, 30

N
names, recognizing 60–61
nappy changes 64, 104–05
neck strength 58
nervous system development 8, 67, 110
neurons 14
newborns
  body language 31
  eyes 26–27
  feeding 36–37, 42–43
  grasp 16, 44–45
  introducing to older sibling 162–63
  movement 30–31
  sight 26
night waking 54–57
no, saying 134–35
numbers, learning 186–87
nurseries 124–25, 158–59
nursery rhymes 86–87, 102

O
object permanence 50, 92, 158
older children
  introducing a new baby 162–63
  jealousy 166–67
  making time for 33, 89, 167
opioids 28
overstimulation, light levels 31
overwhelm
  learning to regulate 142–43
  parents 9, 111
  parties 151
  play 75, 91
  recognizing 29, 53, 63
  tantrums 172
oxytocin 20, 28, 37, 67, 90, 106

P
pain, cries 53
palmar reflex 44–45
parentese 39, 60
parenting
  co-parenting 23, 40–41, 89, 111, 120–21, 140
  emotions 9, 11, 23
  four pillars 9
  good enough approach 10–11, 40
parents
  changes on becoming a parent 22–23
  co-parenting 23, 40–41
  favourite parent 120–21
  hormone changes 22
  overwhelm 9, 111
  premature babies 33
  self-regulation 9, 121, 131, 135, 137, 139, 140, 159, 171, 173
  toddlers understanding feelings 168–69

partners, relationships 23, 40, 41
peekaboo 51, 83, 92–93, 125
perfection, not aiming for 10–11, 40
pets 122–23
phones, children 192–93
phone screens 55
pincer grasp 17, 70
play
   alongside others 19, 154, 157
   bonding 21
   button pressing 126–27
   importance 96–97
   laughter 90–91
   mess 116–17
   outdoors 117, 123
   outside 147, 155, 175, 195
   overwhelm 75
   peekaboo 51, 83, 92–93, 125
   role-playing 114–15, 125, 141, 157, 162, 189
   scribbling and drawing 148–49
pointing 83, 100–101, 145
potty training 105, 141, 182–83
prams, toddler refusal 164–65
prefrontal cortex 118, 146
pregnancy
   connection 20
   feeding reflex development 37
   sound 20, 38
   touch 166
premature babies 32–33, 48, 67
priority setting 23

R

rattles 59
reading 83, 144–45, 169, 187, 197
recognition of parents 16, 29, 38, 50–51
reflexes
   grasp 16, 44–45
   Moro Reflex 34–35
   rooting 30, 31, 36, 37
   startle 34–35, 38, 39
   sucking 36, 45
   swallowing 36
   tongue thrust 46, 47
regression 163
relationships
   being on the same team 23
   intimacy 49
   modelling 157
   reconnecting 40, 41
repetition
   favourite books 144–45
   key to learning 15, 119
   play 97
   speech 19, 61, 73, 112
risk-taking 146–47
road safety 147
role-playing 114–15, 125, 141, 157, 162, 189

rolling over 64–65
rooting reflex 30, 31, 36, 37
routines, creating 77, 111, 119, 173, 195

S

safety
   choking hazards 71
   Christmas 150
   co-sleeping 48–49
   crawling 81
   emotions 28
   feeling safe 28, 29, 110–11, 119
   flying games 75
   household appliance buttons 127
   learning to self-regulate 142–43
   risk-taking 146–47
   starting to move 64
scaffolding 15
screen time
   children 97, 113, 141, 149, 192–93, 196–97
   parents 22, 55, 113, 189, 193, 197
   video calls 197
scribbling 148–49
self-recognition 84–85
self-regulation
   child learning 142–43, 171, 173
   parents 9, 121, 131, 135, 137, 139, 140, 159, 171, 173
senses
   learning 14, 28
   recognition of parents 16, 29, 38, 50–51
sensitivity 142–43, 177
separation anxiety 51, 93, 119, 124–25, 136, 158, 159
sequencing 77, 145
sharing 154–55
siblings
   introducing a new baby 162–63
   jealousy 166–67
   making time for older children 33, 89, 167
sight
   colour development 16, 26–27, 58, 180–81
   focus 58
   newborns 26
   parent recognition 29
   recognition of parents 50
   staring 58–59
sign language 83
singing 33, 83, 86–87, 184–85
sitting, feeding 78, 79
skin to skin contact 29, 33, 53, 57, 67
sleep
   bedtime routines 57, 137
   breastfeeding 106
   co-sleeping 48–49, 88
   dreams 161

   hormones 55
   lullabies 86, 87
   newborns 54–57
   sleep skills 49, 57
   toddler refusal 136–37
slings 35, 53, 163
smell
   parent recognition 29
   recognition of parents 50
smiling 50, 51, 62–63
social skills 156–57
soothing
   toddler bedtimes 137
   weaning off dummies 128–29
sound
   music 61
   parent recognition 16, 20, 29, 38
   parent's heartbeat 57
   rattles 59
   recognition of parents 50
   recognizing own name 60–61
   volume 39
   volume and tempo 102–03
   white noise 32
speech
   babbling 16, 17, 21, 72–73
   bilingualism 190–91
   colours 180–81
   eye contact 61, 189
   first words 18, 82–83, 112–13
   naming things 101
   parentese 39, 60
   recognizing names 60–61
   repetition 19, 61, 73, 112
   saying no 134–35
   sign language 83
   toddlers 19, 188–89
   vocabulary at 24 months 15
   walking 132
spoons 79
squints 59
staring 58–59
startle reflex 34–35, 38, 39
stranger anxiety 98–99, 124
stress
   crying 52, 56
   hormones 28, 52
   hunger 37
   laughter 91
   nervous system development 8
   tantrums 172
sucking reflex 36
Sudden Infant Cot Death 48, 49
support network 22, 41, 111
surprises 151
swaddling 31, 35
swallowing reflex 36
swimming 75
synapses 13, 14

T

tandem feeding 163
tantrums 163, 172–73
taste
  mouthing 70
  parent recognition 29
teeth-brushing 178–79
teething 70
theory of mind 101, 121, 157, 171
thinking, development overview 16–19
thumb-sucking 129
tidying-up 117
tiredness
  crying 53
  movements 30
toilet training 105, 141, 182–83
tongue, sticking out 46–47
touch
  bonding 20, 66–67
  massage 33, 67
  nervous system development 67
  pregnancy 66
  safety 29
toys
  baby gyms 31, 59
  bath time 77
  favourites 138–39
  gifts 151
  reality and imagination 160–61
  rotating 97
  sharing 154–55
  simple 97, 115
travel 140–41
tryptophan 106
tummy time 45, 59, 64
turn-taking 89, 93, 114, 154–55, 167
twins 88–89

V

vestibular system 74
video calls 197
vision *see* sight

W

walking 18, 132–33, 174–75
weaning *see* food
white noise 32
Winnicott, Donald 10

THE AUTHOR

Tanith Carey is an award-winning writer, counsellor, and author of 12 books on parenting and psychology. Her books are published in over 40 countries, including the US, Canada, France, Germany, and China. As a veteran journalist and former US correspondent, Tanith also writes for a wide range of global publications, including *The Guardian*, *The Times*, and *The Spectator*. Her books include the four titles in the *What's My Child Thinking?* series (DK), *The Friendship Maze*, *Taming the Tiger Parent*, and *Girls Uninterrupted: Steps for building stronger girls in a challenging world*. Tanith's speaking engagements have included the Child Mind Institute in Palo Alto, California, and The Cheltenham Science Festival, UK. She holds a Certificate in Therapeutic Skills and Studies from London's Metanoia Institute, where she is training for her Gestalt psychotherapy Masters. Tanith has two children. For a full biography, see www.tanithcarey.com.

THE CONSULTANT

Dr Angharad Rudkin is a clinical psychologist and Associate Fellow of the British Psychological Society, and has worked with families for more than 25 years. She has a therapy practice and consults as well as teaches clinical child psychology. She regularly contributes to the national press and appears on TV and radio. She has three children.

ACKNOWLEDGEMENTS

From the Author As well as my children, Lily and Clio, who are my inspiration, and Dr Rudkin, who is always a joy to work with, I want to thank the past and present researchers, teachers, psychologists and therapists who have created this rich well of understanding of baby development, on which this book is based. By truly trying to understand what our children are trying to tell us, and attuning to their needs, right from the start, it's possible to create a happier, more peaceful world.

From the Consultant Thank you to Tanith and all at DK for recognising the importance of these first 750 days. Thank you also to the new parents who spoke to me about their experiences. And a huge thank you to my own babies, who continue to teach me about love and life every day.

From the Publisher DK would like to thank Athena Stacy for editorial support, Francesco Piscitelli for proofreading, and Ruth Ellis for indexing.

DK LONDON
Senior Acquisitions Editor Zara Anvari
Editor Jasmin Lennie
Senior Designer Glenda Fisher
Production Editor David Almond
Production Controller Samantha Cross
Publishing Coordinator Emily Cannings
Art Director Maxine Pedliham
Publishing Director Stephanie Jackson

Editorial Clare Double
Design Tom Forge, Emma Forge
Illustration Céleste Wallaert
Jacket Designer Eleanor Ridsdale

First published in Great Britain in 2025 by
Dorling Kindersley Limited
20 Vauxhall Bridge Road,
London SW1V 2SA

The authorised representative in the EEA is
Dorling Kindersley Verlag GmbH. Arnulfstr. 124,
80636 Munich, Germany

Copyright © 2025 Dorling Kindersley Limited
A Penguin Random House Company
10 9 8 7 6 5 4 3 2 1
001–345323–Nov/2025

All rights reserved.
No part of this publication may be reproduced, stored in or introduced into a retrieval system, or transmitted, in any form, or by any means (electronic, mechanical, photocopying, recording, or otherwise), without the prior written permission of the copyright owner.

DK values and supports copyright. Thank you for respecting intellectual property laws by not reproducing, scanning or distributing any part of this publication by any means without permission. By purchasing an authorised edition, you are supporting writers and artists and enabling DK to continue to publish books that inform and inspire readers. No part of this publication may be used or reproduced in any manner for the purpose of training artificial intelligence technologies or systems. In accordance with Article 4(3) of the DSM Directive 2019/790, DK expressly reserves this work from the text and data mining exception.

A CIP catalogue record for this book
is available from the British Library.
ISBN: 978-0-2417-2081-3

Printed and bound in China

www.dk.com

This book was made with Forest Stewardship Council™ certified paper – one small step in DK's commitment to a sustainable future. Learn more at www.dk.com/uk/information/sustainability

---

Disclaimer
The information in this book has been compiled as general guidance on the specific subjects addressed. It is not a substitute and not to be relied on for medical, healthcare, or pharmaceutical professional advice. If you have any concerns about any aspect of your child's behaviour, health, or wellbeing, please seek professional advice. Please seek medical advice before changing, stopping, or starting any of your child's medical treatment. So far as the author is aware the information given is correct and up to date as of March 2025. Practice, laws, and regulations all change and the reader should obtain up-to-date professional advice on any such issues.
The author and publishers disclaim, as far as the law allows, any liability arising directly or indirectly from the use or misuse of the information contained in this book.